Back in School

A Guide for Adult Learners

By
Charles J. Shields

CAREER PRESS
180 Fifth Avenue
P.O. Box 34
Hawthorne, NJ 07507
1-800-CAREER-1
201-427-0229 (outside U.S.)
FAX: 201-427-2037

Copyright © 1994 by Charles J. Shields

BACK IN SCHOOL

ISBN 1-56414-124-1, $11.95

Cover design by The Gottry Communications Group, Inc.

Printed in the U.S.A. by Book-mart Press

To order this title by mail, please include price as noted above, $2.50 handling per order, and $1.00 for each book ordered. Send to: Career Press, Inc., 180 Fifth Ave., P.O. Box 34, Hawthorne, NJ 07507

Or call toll-free 1-800-CAREER-1 (Canada: 201-427-0229) to order using VISA or MasterCard, or for further information on books from Career Press.

Library of Congress Cataloging-in-Publication Data

Shields, Charles J., 1951-
    Back in school : a guide for adult learners / by Charles J. Shields.
        p.   cm.
    Includes index.
    ISBN 1-56414-124-1 : $11.95
    1. College student orientation. 2. Adult learning. 3. Study skills. I. Title.
    LB2343.32.S55   1994
    374'.973--dc20   94-19988
                                                                CIP

Dedication

To Guadalupe—
te amo, mi esposa

Acknowledgments

This book is better than it would have been because of generous help from Gail White, guidance department secretary; Dennis O'Brien, friend and librarian; and Eleanor Steiner, career specialist—all at Homewood-Flossmoor High School. Also, Annie Curtis provided the first-rate interviews with students and professionals: I'm grateful.

Finally, Lauren and Andrew have learned to accept their dad's odd preoccupation with sitting at the computer—writing, writing, writing. Thanks, bunny-pumpkins.

Contents

Chapter 1

Is Now a Good Time to Go Back to School?

"Your total for tuition and fees is $320," said the woman in the teller's window.

"Three hundred and twenty bucks," I thought to myself. "And I've still got to get books, pencils—all that stuff." I wrote a check and recorded the amount in my register, noticing how it stuck out in the list of day-to-day "survival" entries: mortgage, groceries, cash for gas, and so on. What should I call this entry? Dad the Undergrad?

"This probably isn't the best idea I've ever had in my life," I mumbled as I passed some students 20 years younger than myself on my way out the door.

But outside, it was an ideal September afternoon: leaves changing to gold, and sunlight tumbling down from a bowl of blue sky.

Looking out over the campus, I couldn't help but feel excited in spite of my doubts. I'd done it! The first step was over. Whatever else might happen, I was bearing down on my dreams.

And as it turned out, going back to school *was* one of the best ideas I've ever had: I read books for class that tuned up my thinking and outlook; I participated in discussions where I said important things that surprised even me; I made new friends who had similar goals and who made me feel welcome in the community of learning. Education defines us, points our compass needle back in the right direction, and opens all kinds of doors leading to an enriched life: intellectually, emotionally, financially.

Are you thinking about going back to school? Enrolling in college classes; signing up for a series of workshops; participating in telecourses via satellite; or taking correspondence courses by mail, for instance? If you're still on the fence, still wavering about taking the plunge, I have two words of advice for you:

Do it.

And you don't have to rely on only my word, either. Listen to the experiences of a few persons who put their education on hold for awhile, and then heard the school bell ring for them again—sometimes years later.

Ten times the understanding

"There's a reason for your biological clock," says 48-year-old Sue Brown. "At 50, you shouldn't be taking care of babies."

For 15 years, Sue ran a day-care business out of her home, adding a significant amount of money to the family income every month. But then, she said, "I started feeling frustrated—always rolling up the rugs so the kids wouldn't spill on them, making sure that valuable things were put away in the closet—I love children, and I'm good with them, but it got to be too much."

When she was 18, Sue had planned to get a college degree right after high school. And she did go to a major state university—for two weeks. "I was overwhelmed, intimidated. I just didn't want to be there," she said. She dropped out; worked in a gift store; then in a bank for several years, until she married at 24.

Now she has three children—two of whom are grown—and it was her son, a sophomore in college, "who took his mother by the hand and led her through the 'terrors' of registering for school," said Sue. Her goal? To receive a certificate as an interpreter for the deaf.

"I'm so positive about it," she said, finishing up her first semester of Monday and Wednesday night classes at a local community college. "I just know this is going to work for me."

Some nights, Sue runs into her former next-door neighbor and close friend, Vivian Feigenbaum.

Vivian, 36, met her future husband while still in high school and married him shortly after graduating. She worked as a dental assistant for seven years, "just putting off the idea of school entirely," she said. "I was afraid of it, and I thought, 'I'm making money—so what?' "

Then came three children, two right in a row, and when her third one was born, she realized, "Something is missing." Not long after that, she and her husband divorced.

The idea of going back to school for a two-year degree in dental hygiene had occurred to her while she was still married. However, she says, being divorced and older than some students in class has put a spin on her education that ultimately works to her advantage: "First, being a single parent created immediate financial need. I've received a lot of help paying for school. Second, I'm getting a real kick out of this because I waited—I'm taking it a lot more seriously. I don't go out and party, I go home and study. And my understanding is 10 times what it was when I was in high school."

What about being older than many students? Does it matter?

"That was a fear of mine at the beginning. Actually, about half the students in the class are my age or older," says Vivian. "There's sort of a peer relationship with the instructors. They're more than teachers—they're friends."

Finally, there's Dave Simpson, the potential scientist who dropped out to drive a truck for 20 years.

Dave was a National Merit Finalist in high school in 1969, a top academic honor that garnered him scholarships to a number of high-powered universities around the country. He finished his B.S. in mathematics at one of them, and had completed a number of the fundamental courses for a graduate degree when, he recalls, "the money just ran out. I started taking odd jobs to pay for the tuition, and then one of them—truck driving—put me in an income category way above what other people my age were earning, so I quit school. 'Wait'll I get ahead a little—till I'm really settled in,' I thought. 'I'll go back.' "

"Settling in" came much later than he thought. Now owning his first home, and newly married at 39, Dave has finished some refresher courses in math at a community college. His grades were As. Next stop: a major university known for turning out what he's always wanted to be—a Ph.D. in physics.

A banquet of educational opportunities

Your story might be similar. Or it might be completely different. In any case, realize that there are plenty of returning students, just like you, flocking to classes and eager to learn.

"We could almost run the university just at night and still stay open," says Thomas B. Abramson, director of admissions at DePaul University in Chicago. "Our night programs for executives and returning students are booming." Overall, the median age of students in college is 24; however, according to the Census Bureau's latest count, well over a quarter of a million Americans enrolled in college courses are age 50 and older. Thousands more are auditing classes, forming retiree study groups, attending university lectures, and joining travel-study programs.

And that's just the tip of the iceberg.

As new groups are seeking career services, new agencies are emerging to attend to unique and different concerns. Colleges and universities are expanding career services for adults coming or returning to school, but these students alone account for only one-fifth—12 million—of the total number of adults being educated today.

Forty-six million adults are being educated by other agencies or by employers. The federal government, for example, offers educational opportunities through the military, equity legislation for women and minorities, programs for attracting women into nontraditional occupations, national and state information systems, reemployment programs, displaced homemaker centers and college reentry programs.

Business and industry alone spend between $30 and $40 billion on the education and training of adults. And these adults are not seeking more of the same services provided to adolescents, but services unique to their own needs. Career-planning services in the workplace, outplacement centers, employee assistance programs that include career services, assessment centers in private businesses—even in shopping centers—are meeting a demand by adults for new career- and life-planning services.

On the other hand, some people enroll in classes, workshops, and seminars just because it can be fun.

"I knew very little about science—not much more than a high school student," says Sue Detrich, 79. "But the history of science was one of the most interesting courses I've ever taken." Offered through a cooperative agreement between a local university, a synagogue and the Elder Hostel organization, the class was eight weeks, and Sue says "There was plenty of gray hair among the students." The next class she enrolled in at the same location was an overview of the history of Native Americans. "These are things I've always been interested in, but never had to the opportunity to study," she said.

In fact, many nontraditional students come back to school to complete educational pursuits they began years before as traditional students. They may have dropped out of education for a number of reasons, including financial considerations, competing responsibilities and lack of focus, motivation and maturity. Other major reasons that adults return to college include family life transitions—marriage, divorce, death—changes in leisure patterns and self-fulfillment.

Some researchers have proposed a "triggers and transitions" theory to explain an adult's mid-life decision to return to school. *Transitions* (the movement from one status to another) require new knowledge, skills and/or credentials that often lead people back to college. *Triggers* are events that precipitate the timing of an adult's decision to return to school—most frequently career events and family changes.

Two researchers identified eight primary motivations for nontraditional women students to decide to pursue an undergraduate degree:

- self-improvement
- self-actualization
- vocational
- role
- family
- social
- humanitarian
- knowledge

The impact of women on educational institutions and the paid labor force has been significant. In 1950, fewer than 5 percent of all women 25 and older possessed college degrees. In 1980, 13 percent did. "Older" women (35 and up) outnumber older men by almost two to one in their return to institutions of higher education, and the enrollment of both older groups has increased to 36.8 percent in five years. Women's pursuit of professional degrees also has sharply increased in the last three decades; for example, from 4 percent to 30 percent in the field of law.

In the labor force, the number of women has increased 109 percent since 1960, compared to 36 percent for men. By 1995, 80 percent of women aged 20 to 45 are predicted to be working in the paid labor force. Women with children under age 6 have increased their participation from 19 percent in 1960 to 50 percent in 1983.

Both men and women, however, understand this workplace reality: more education tends to bring more income. Changing job requirements or career changes often force adults to get additional education to survive or advance in the job market. According to researcher W. F. Brazziel (1989), "the ever upward progression of an educated adult population and work force and increased educational requirements for high-paying jobs—might be the single most powerful factor" in the continued influx of adult students on college campuses.

More education, more money

It's no secret. High school dropouts are more likely to have low-paying jobs with little advancement potential, while workers in occupations requiring higher levels of education have higher incomes. And here's something about tomorrow's jobs you can bank on: three out of the four fastest-growing occupational groups from now until 2005 will be executive, administrative and managerial; professional speciality; and technicians and related support occupations. These occupations—such as credit managers, teachers, paralegals, engineering technicians, health services managers and thousands more—generally require the highest levels of education and skill, and will make up an increasing proportion of new jobs. The fourth area of job growth will be in the service-producing sector as well, but these jobs—cashiers, retail sales workers, waiters—require less education and pay lower wages.

The "losers" in the coming decade, the U.S. Bureau of Labor Statistics is predicting, will be the occupations requiring the least formal education. The impact of office and factory automation, changes in consumer demand, and substitution of imports for domestic products are expected to cause employment to stagnate or decline in jobs for apparel and manufacturing workers, miners and machinery operators, for example.

In fact, if you're interested in a rundown of where the good-paying jobs will be the next decade, here it is:

The long-term shift in the U.S. economy from goods-producing to service-producing employment will continue. Service-producing industries—including transportation, communications and utilities; retail and wholesale trade; services; government; and finance, insurance and real estate—are expected to account for approximately 23 million of the 24.6 million new jobs created by the year 2005. Within this big grouping, the services division—which includes health, business and educational services—will contain 16 of the 20 fastest-growing industries, and 12 of the 20 industries adding the most jobs.

Let's have a look at them.

Where the jobs are

Employment in the health services industries is projected to grow from 8.9 million to 12.8 million. Improvements in medical technology, and a growing and aging population (the population 85 or older will grow more than three times as fast as the total population) will increase the demand for health services. Employment in home health care services—the fastest growing industry in the U.S. economy—nursing homes, and offices and clinics of physicians and other health practitioners—is projected to increase the most rapidly during the next decade.

Business services will also generate many jobs. Employment is expected to grow from 5.2 million to 7.6 million. This industry includes one of the fastest-growing in the economy: computer and data processing services. Business services's rapid growth stems from advances in technology, worldwide trends toward office and factory automation, and increases in demand from business firms, government agencies and individuals.

Third, education, both public and private, added 2.3 million jobs to the 9.4 million in 1990. This increase reflects population growth and, in turn, rising enrollments projected for elementary, secondary and postsecondary schools. The elementary-age school population (ages 5 to 13) will rise by 3.8 million by 2005, the secondary school age (14 to 17) by 1.4 million. In addition, continued rising enrollments of older (that's you!), foreign and part-time students are expected to enhance employment in post-secondary education. Not all of the increase in employment in education, however, will be for teachers; teacher aides, counselors and administrative staff are projected to increase, too.

That's where the better salaries will be: in providing health, business and educational services. But employers in these industries will be expecting relatively high levels of education or training.

After all, they can afford to be demanding. In recent years, the level of educational attainment of the labor force has risen dramatically. Between 1975 and 1990, the proportion of the labor force age 25 to 64 with at least one year of college increased from 33 percent to 47 percent, while the proportion with four years of college or more increased from 18 percent to 26 percent.

That means better-educated workers coming on line, and especially ones in their prime: ages 45 to 54. These workers should account for 24 percent of the labor force by the year 2005, up from 16 percent in 1990. In fact, the number of older workers, 55 and above, is projected to grow about twice as fast as the total labor force by 2005. Why? Because improvements in health care and revised attitudes about the length of a person's worklife will mean more workers in the Baby Boom generation, which makes up about one-third of the population, staying on the job longer.

Another reason there will be more older workers is because women continue to join the labor force in growing numbers. Women were only 40 percent of the labor force in 1975; by 2005, they are expected to constitute 47 percent. And the financial rewards seem to be there, at least in business. In 1980, 35 percent of corporate women officers made vice president or above; in 1992, it was 72 percent.

So if you're 30 or older, you've got a lot of competition: There are plenty of workers in the economy who could fill that job you've got your eye on. One of the best ways to give yourself an edge, or make yourself more promotable in the field you're already in, is to stay current on professional developments; make yourself flexible; be prepared for change. In other words, go back for more education.

Here's how to do it, step-by-step.

A checklist for your options

- *Decide what type of education you want.* If your goal is to obtain professional credentials in your field, you may need a bachelor's or even a graduate degree. If your field requires only partial college training, you might want to aim for an associate's degree. Or, if you just want to acquire specific skills, a continuing education program or a few professional seminars might be right for you.

- *Find out what's available in your area.* If your community has an educational resource center, you may be able to obtain catalogs and brochures about your community's educational institutions all in one place. Try your local library. But the most direct way is to phone area schools, identify yourself as a prospective student and ask for their course catalogs. (see Chapter 3: "How Do I Get Started On My Plans?")

- *Decide how much time you can devote to school.* If you're working full-time, your choices are independent study or evening or weekend classes. But which would be right for you? Are some evenings better than others? Can you attend school part-time for several years, taking semesters off now and then? If you have children, can you take a pass on courses during the summer? On the other hand, can you accelerate during the summer months through intensive mini-sessions or seminars? But keep in mind that for every hour of class time, you'll probably have to spend at least two hours reading, studying, or doing research. Don't forget to include travel time back and forth to campus. So how many classes can you realistically handle at one time?

- *Think about the kind of educational climate you prefer.* What kinds of courses would be best for you. Hands-on? Discussion? Laboratory? Large lecture? Small group? And what kinds of faculty members are you looking for? Professors trained in the academic world, or ones who spend part of their time working in your profession?

- *Would remedial help in English and math assist you?* Do you think you might need special advising or counseling along the way? Tutoring? A support group? Many colleges and commercial schools offer these opportunities, so ask about them. After all, it could be you previously attended school when learning disabilities were unknown. Or perhaps your absence from the schoolroom means your skills need sharpening-up. As part of your planning, don't be embarassed to seek help. As your teachers used to tell you, "The only 'dumb' question is the one that isn't asked."

- *Discuss your goals with an admissions representative.* After reading about the programs available to you, call admissions offices of the ones that interest you. Don't be bashful. Ask the rep about the features you'd like in your education; the information you've read in the catalog; the experiences of other adult learners and their career paths. Arrange to take a tour of the campus and sit in on a few classes. And this is especially important: Talk to other students. Ask them about their experiences—what would they recommend if they were just starting like you?

- *Look into transferring credit.* If you've attended college-level classes in the past, or in some cases, if you have what colleges call "life experiences," you may be able to transfer the credit to a degree program. Call or write for copies of your transcripts or records—see which courses can be counted toward you new program.

- *Develop a financing package.* Now comes the question of money. You'll have to estimate your educational costs, then figure out a strategy for meeting them. The state may make higher education grants available to mature students. Or, long-term student loans at reduced interest rates are available in all states. Also, individual schools may have special awards or scholarships to attract qualified adult students. In any event, the admissions representative will be able to provide you with worksheets detailing costs and financial aid, or applications for financial aid. (See Chapter 4: "How Will I Pay for More Education?")

- *Apply to the school.* Many colleges and commercial schools offer streamlined application packages for part-time, adult learners. You'll probably have to submit a three- or four-page application describing your past education, job experiences and career activities. There probably won't be an interview, unless you request one, or an exam.

But we're getting ahead of ourselves a bit. Read on and you'll learn how to make your educational plans and goals come true, step-by-step, because right now is a good time to go back to school.

Chapter 2

Is a College Degree My Only Option?

Did you know that 60 percent of jobs *don't* require a four-year college degree? That's right—we tend to think there are two end-points in education: a high school diploma or a college degree.

But that overlooks a lot of educational opportunities in be-tween: some of them geared for professional advancement; some designed for personal enrichment.

Think about you own neighborhood, for instance. How many of these learning sites are available?

- a museum
- a bookstore
- a library
- a major metropolitan newspaper
- a park district
- a gallery
- a zoo
- a club
- a church/synogogue
- a community college

You could occupy most of your free time just learning—some of it job-related, much of it just for enjoyment.

But time and your responsibilities prevent you from becoming a full-time student-at-large. So like any busy person, you want to maximize your efforts by devoting them to programs of study that will bring concrete results. These results might include a certificate authenticating your expertise; or a license to practice; or an official transcript of credits earned.

Realize, however, that these kinds of credentials are not available solely from four-year colleges or universities. Depending on what point you're at in your education, and where you want to go personally or professionally, a range of opportunities are open to you.

Let's start at the beginning.

Back to the future: High school

First of all, do you need to finish high school before you can even consider additional education?

If you've been out of high school for some time, without a diploma, look into the General Educational Development (GED) Test. It's a battery of five comprehensive examinations in social studies, science, writing, reading and mathematics. Developed during World War II, the GED program was first used to help returning service men and women complete their high school education. Since then, millions of Americans have received their high school equivalency certificates by passing the tests. It's the first step to going on to college, or business or trade schools; satisfying educational qualifications for government employment; or fulfilling requirements for state or local licensing boards.

The GED tests are based on skills, rather than on the mere recall of facts from various subjects. They measure learning and skill development that result from experience, from reading, and from other nontraditional avenues.

The exams are developed under the supervision of the Commission on Accreditation of the American Council on Education, and updated by the Educational Testing Service (ETS). Each State Department of Education establishes the guidelines for administering them, and for assigning scores. It also fixes age, residency and previous high school enrollment requirements (for example, in some states, a person must be 18 or out of high school for a year before sitting for the exams). In most states, a passing score for each part of the GED exam is 35; a passing score for all five parts of the test must total 225.

But your best bet for finding out the specifics about the GED exams in your area is this: Call a local community college. Speak to an admissions counselor. It's likely that the college offers GED test-prep classes to refresh your memory, review facts and sharpen your test-taking skills. These are worth the time.

On the other hand, you don't need to attend classes at all—at least not in the formal sense. You can also earn a high school diploma through the mail.

"Dear Professor..."

Each year millions of Americans enroll in correspondence study. They do so for many reasons—to advance their careers, increase their incomes, obtain better jobs or simply to learn something new. Correspondence study allows a practical, convenient method of accomplishing any these objectives.

The method has many advantages—flexibility being the primary one. For example, you can enroll at any time and study at home. Because there are no classes or semester deadlines, you study at your own pace. Where and when to study is up to you: study day or night, on weekends, in your spare time or during vacations, at work, at home or while traveling. You may complete a one-hour course in as little as six weeks, or take a year or more: the choice is yours.

In addition, correspondence study permits the use of other materials—cassettes, group study outlines, telecourses, videotapes, films, slides and computer disks—in addition to the regular text-book and the exchange of lessons via mail.

Two institutions that offer high school diplomas through correspondence study are the American School in Chicago, Illinois, and Home Study International in Silver Spring, Maryland. Both are accredited by national organizations such as the Accrediting Commission of the National Home Study Council (NHSC), Washington, D.C., the Illinois Office of Education and the Maryland State Department of Education.

American School is considered the world's largest high school with a current student body of around 40,000. Over 4,500 public, private and parochial high schools use American School's wide variety of correspondence courses to supplement their own study with courses not available in the smaller schools. *The diplomas awarded are actual high school diplomas, not GED equivalency certificates.*

In addition to the standard high school courses—English, math, history and science—students may choose from nearly 80 offerings such as machine shop courses, childcare, electronics, automotive and diesel courses, consumer economics, foreign languages, science, ecology and oceanography, drafting, carpentry and blueprint reading, office skills, and many more. Each course comes complete with text and study guide.

The time you spend in a program will depend on the number of courses transferred in from previous study. Course credit and dollar credit is granted for each subject already completed. Students who are highly motivated are able to finish a year of high school work in as little as five or six months. Upon completion, students take an exam, which is individually graded and returned.

There are two programs available:

- General High School Course (eight units of required study and eight units of electives)
- College Preparatory Course (11 units of required study and five units of electives)

The General Course is recommended for persons who wish basic training in a particular field. Many junior colleges and technical schools accept students with this diploma. The College Preparatory Course is for persons with a college program in mind. Over 800 universities have accepted American School graduates. Here's the address:

American School
850 East 58th Street
Chicago, IL 60637
312-947-3300

Home Study International (HSI) has also helped thousands of people achieve their educational goals. In addition to the high school diploma, HSI also offers a complete educational program including preschool, kindergarten, elementary, junior high, college and adult education.

As is the case with most accredited correspondence study, each course offered by HSI has been written by an expert in the field and is graded by a qualified teacher:

Home Study International
P.O. Box 4437
Silver Spring, MD 20914-4437
800-394-GROW (4769)

But wait, there are also three universities that offer high school diplomas through correspondence study, which are worth checking into because of their reasonable costs:

Brigham Young University
Department of Independent Study
Provo, UT 84602
801-378-2868

Note: Students who take high school independent study courses toward a diploma through Brigham Young University receive their diploma through a cooperating local school district.

University of Arkansas
Center for Continuing Education
Department of Independent Study
#2 University Center
Fayetteville, AR 72701
501-575-3647
800-632-0035, ext. 3647 (toll-free for Arkansas residents)

University of Nebraska-Lincoln
Independent Study High School
269 NCCE
Lincoln, NB 68583
402-472-1926

Call the registrar at the phone number listed for each institution and ask for printed information about earning a high school diploma through the mail.

Correspondence schools: The big picture

Earning a high school diploma through the mail is just one possibility, however. There are more than 400 correspondence schools in the United States offering hundreds of courses. A few even grant accredited academic degrees.

But do your homework first before enrolling in any program. Find out about cost, length of study, what happens if you fail to complete the course, and whether the institution can guarantee that the credits are transferable.

Credits earned through correspondence study may or may not be accepted as transfer credits by a college or university to fulfill degree requirements, for example. If you plan to transfer correspondence credits toward a degree program, it's your responsibility to discover beforehand whether the number of courses and the hours will be accepted by the institution from which you eventually intend to graduate.

There are generally two types of correspondence courses: vocational and academic.

Vocational home study courses are those leading to expertise in specialized fields such as television repair, locksmithing, scriptwriting, broadcasting, interior design, auto mechanics, landscaping, hotel management, foreign languages, clerical skills and so on. As a rule, credits earned in this type of study cannot be applied toward college degrees. Course length ranges from a few weeks to over four years of study. While some schools may have fewer that 500 students, various armed forces correspondence institutes have enrollments of more than 500,000 students.

Interested? Get a free copy of the "Directory of Accredited Home Study Schools," available from the National Home Study Council, 1601 18th Street, N.W., Washington, D.C. 20009.

If it's academic courses designed specifically to earn college credits you're interested in, then look into programs accredited by the Independent Study Division of the National University Continuing

Education Association (NUCEA). NUCEA is a professional organization of approximately 70 colleges and universities offering correspondence courses. All NUCEA institutions are members of their respective regional educational accrediting associations.

Specific information concerning NUCEA correspondence courses is available in a publication entitled *The Independent Study Catalog: The NUCEA Guide to Independent Study Through Correspondence Instruction*. (Peterson's Guides, P.O. Box 2123, Princeton, New Jersey 08543. 800-338-3282.)

This guide lists approximately 10,000 correspondence courses at the high school, college and graduate levels: from abnormal psychology, to entrepreneurship, to nutrition, to writing for television.

Another very large, but easy-to-use, correspondence study reference is *The MacMillan Guide to Correspondence Study,* carried in the reference section of most local libraries.

But before you put down your money for a correspondence course, answer this: Can you pass a test that would earn you college credit right away?

Credit by examination

Over 2,000 colleges and universities in the United States and Canada award college credit based entirely on examinations.

By taking an equivalency examination, as it's called, you can demonstrate college-level learning you've acquired outside the classroom. In addition, credit by examination saves considerable time and money by allowing you to enter a college program at an advanced level. Satisfactory examination scores may qualify you for higher-level courses in particular fields of interest, and in some cases, may fulfill professional licensing and certification requirements.

But if you look into earning credit by examination, it's important that you first check with school officials: policies regarding equivalency examinations differ from one school to another. Ask:

- Will the school grant credit for equivalency exams? For which ones?

- Will the school grant the maximum number of credits for exams?

• Will the school charge for credit transferred to the college transcript? (Some schools will add credit to your transcript at no charge; some charge half-tuition or more).

Here's a summary of credit-by-exam programs:

CLEP

There are several types of equivalency exams, but by far the most widely accepted credit-by-exam program in the country is CLEP, the College-Level Examination Program. CLEP exams were first introduced in 1967. More than 200,000 individuals each year "CLEP out" of classes, because nearly three-quarters of all accredited institutions of higher education award credit for satisfactory scores on CLEP exams. CLEP examinations are offered by the College Board, a nonprofit membership organization that provides tests and other educational services for students, schools and colleges. The membership includes more than 2,700 colleges and universities, as well as secondary schools and education associations.

CLEP exams focus on the first two years of undergraduate courses offered in most colleges. They're divided into two areas: General Exams, which cover five broad areas of general education—English composition, humanities, mathematics, natural sciences, social sciences and history; and second—Subject Exams, which consist of 30 separate tests offered in history and social sciences, foreign languages, composition and literature, science and mathematics, and business.

Each 90-minute test is multiple-choice. From one to six college credits may be earned for satisfactory scores; as many as 30 credits (or the equivalent of one year of college) may be earned on the five General Exams. The fee for a CLEP General or Subject Examination is $38. No more than four 90-minute tests may be taken in any one day. Tests may be repeated after six months have passed.

Test centers—there are more than 1,200—may schedule exams at any time. Candidates should contact the center they wish to use for dates and times. The exception is the CLEP English Composition essay exam, which is given four times a year: October, January, April and June. Special testing arrangements are available to persons who live more than 150 miles from a test center or outside the U.S.; for civilians at overseas military bases; for members of the armed forces; and for persons with special needs.

Scores are confidential: Results will be released only with your permission (they're kept on file for 20 years). Individual scores may be sent to one or more of the participating colleges, or to an employer or organization.

Information about the program plus a list of all CLEP test centers are in two free publications—"Make Learning Pay with CLEP," and "CLEP Colleges: Where You Can Be Tested/Where You Can Get Credit." (CLEP, CN 6601, Princeton, NJ 08541-6601, 215-750-8420)

To help prepare for CLEP exams, the College Board offers *Guide to the CLEP Examination*, which describes each CLEP test and provides sample test questions and answers. It's available in bookstores.

PEP

Another program for receiving college credits is the Proficiency Examination Program (PEP) examinations offered in the state of New York by Regents College. Outside New York, PEP examinations are offered by the American College Testing Program (ACT).

PEP exams are offered in 42 college subjects in the broad areas of arts and sciences, business, education and nursing. The majority are objective exams, but many of those on business are essay tests. Most are three hours long; the essay tests are four hours in length. PEP tests are administered six times a year in two-day sessions at about 175 testing centers and military bases (through DANTES) across the nation. Fees for individual tests range from $45 to $55 for multiple-choice tests to $140 for essay tests.

There are free study guides. Also available free is a booklet entitled "Preparing To Do Your Best On ACT PEP Examinations." For a complete packet of information write:

(in New York State)
Regents College
1450 Western Avenue
Albany, NY 12203

(outside New York State)
PEP Operations
American College Testing Program
P.O. Box 4014
Iowa City, IA 52433

DANTES tests

DANTES Subject Standardized Tests (DSST) is a testing program developed by the Educational Testing Service (ETS) under
contract to the Department of Defense.

The tests were created as opportunities for members of the
armed forces to obtain college credit for knowledge acquired outside classrooms. Now, however, the tests are available to civilians
as well as military students. Hundreds of two- and four-year
colleges and universities across the country accept credit earned
for satisfactory scores.

Approximately 50 different tests are included in the program.
Each one covers materials commonly taught in a one-semester
freshman or sophomore college course. There are tests that cover,
for example:

- *Business subjects* (marketing, business, risk and insurance, business math, personnel/human resource management, organizational behavior, etc.)

- *Technical subjects* (basic technical drafting, fundamentals
  of electronics, basic automotive service, introduction to
  carpentry, technical writing, introduction to computers
  using Basic, and more)

- *Social sciences* (life-span developmental psychology,
  criminal justice, introduction to law enforcement, general
  anthropology, etc.)

- *Physical Sciences* (physical geology, principles of physical
  science, and others)

- *Languages* (German, Spanish and Italian), and other
  subjects.

Tests are untimed but generally take about 90 minutes. There is no fixed schedule and tests can be administered at any time convenient for the test administrator and the student.

A list of the tests is available, plus fact sheets for each test giving the content of the test; sample questions and list of texts for preparation; and a list of schools that administer DSST's and accept scores for credit. For free information, write DANTES Program, Mail Stop 3/X, Educational Testing Service, Princeton, NJ 08541. When requesting fact sheets, indicate which tests you're interested in.

In addition, DANTES makes available to military personnel, free of charge, approximately 100 proficiency examinations for college credit. Service members may take the ACT PEP examinations, CLEP General and Subject examinations, and DANTES Subject Standardized Tests (DSST's) toward fulfillment of degree requirements.

Recent additions to the DANTES credit-by-examination program are the Automotive Service Excellence and the Institute for Certified Computer Professional (ICCP) Associate Computer Professional examinations. The majority of colleges use minimum passing examination scores and credit recommendations as set by ACE. For details contact a Base Education Office.

Ready, set, test

You can prepare yourself for most national standardized tests like the GED, CLEP, PEP and others. Review manuals can be found in college bookstores, regular bookstores, public libraries, and education service centers.

In addition, there is a national network of over 150 examination preparation centers (the Stanley H. Kaplan Educational Centers), which prepare individuals for about 30 different kinds of standardized examinations. These centers are located throughout the United States, Puerto Rico, Canada and Seoul, Korea. Call 800-KAP-TEST or write to Stanley H. Kaplan Educational Center Ltd., 810 Seventh Avenue, 22nd Floor, New York, NY 10019 for more information.

Credit for living

Life is a great teacher, and you may be able to garner some academic credit for what you've learned over the years, provided you can document your experiences and the knowledge you gained. Both military experience and experiential learning—knowledge you've picked up on your own—are two resources in your background you might be able to apply to any program of study. Read on and find out how you can blend what you've already learned with what you still want to know.

Credit for military experience

Within the military lies a vast wealth of practical experience and education, for example. If you have this background you may wish to consider converting some of it into college credits.

The Center for Adult Learning and Educational Credentials of the American Council on Education (ACE) evaluates for academic credit all military technical training courses. These courses are offered by all branches of the service including the United States Coast Guard. Academic credit recommendations are also available for Army, Navy, Marine Corps and Coast Guard enlisted and warrant officer job specialties, and Navy limited duty officer specialties. The credit recommendations developed by the ACE are recognized and accepted by most colleges and universities, and may count toward a college degree. Additionally, the Air Force recognizes its own technical training toward the associate degree requirements of the Community College of the Air Force (CCAF), which is an accredited two-year degree-granting institution.

Credit for experiential learning

Some colleges and universities award college credits or advanced standing to persons for knowledge acquired outside the traditional classroom.

But it's important to understand that college credit is not granted for the experience alone, but for the knowledge gained from the experience. For instance, a person would not be granted college credits simply on the basis of having been employed in sales for 10 years. He may, however, be granted credit for those learning activities in which he participated as a salesperson such as in-service training, workshops, seminars, motivational clinics, conventions, teaching and training responsibilities, product demonstrations, business trips, in-depth reading in a specialized area, and other learning activities.

Most schools require that life learning experiences be officially documented and submitted to the school in the form of a life experience portfolio. A few schools offer life experience (experiential) courses or workshops to assist the student in developing his or her own portfolio.

Listed below are eight major categories of experiences that may yield learning that qualifies for college credits in nontraditional degree programs:

- *Work* (skills and activities performed on the job including military service activities)

- *Homemaking* (home management, planning and budgeting, child-rearing/education, gourmet cooking, nutrition)

- *Volunteer work* (community service, church/synogogue activities, political activities, service organization activities, social work, youth counseling)

- *Noncredit courses* (adult education courses, correspondence courses, seminars, lectures, company in-service training, conferences, conventions, military service courses, television/radio/computer courses, workshops, clinics)

- *Travel* (study tours, business trips, significant vacations, extended leaves/assignments in foreign countries)

- *Recreation and hobbies* (may include a multitude of leisure-time activities such as sports, aviation, music, community theater, writing, public speaking, arts, crafts, design, landscaping, gardening, sewing, carpentry, etc.)

- *Independent reading, viewing, listening* (specialized or intensive study via books, articles, radio/television programs)

- *Conversations with experts* (significant meetings and discussions)

There are several forms of documentation that are appropriate in a life experience portfolio. "Letters of verification" from employers are the most common. Other forms include resumes, licenses—pilot, real estate, day care, and so on, reports, newspaper articles, commendations, awards and citations, certificates and diplomas, military records, copies of examinations taken, course outlines or syllabi, films or taped presentations, job descriptions, product samples, works of art, designs and blueprints, exhibitions, written or edited manuscripts, photographs, copies of speeches, programs of performances, recitals, and bills of sale.

Faculty members will evaluate your life experience portfolios. Credit is granted according to how thoroughly you describe or document the experience and the learning.

Keep in mind that preparing a portfolio takes work. However, considering that colleges are allowing as much as two years of college credits (this varies between schools), the substantial savings in both time and money can make the effort worthwhile. Another benefit derived from preparing a portfolio is this: the process will help you recognize and appraise your particular skills and knowledge. This can be a great advantage in the development of a degree plan.

For help in preparing and submitting a life experience portfolio to a college, there is an excellent guidebook available: *Earn College Credit For What You Know* by Lois Lamdin. It contains information on identifying appropriate learning experiences, plus step-by-step instructions for assembling a portfolio. Other chapters describe evaluation procedures, and there's a list of colleges offering assessment of prior learning opportunities. (Council for Adult & Experiential Learning (CAEL) 223 West Jackson, Suite 510, Chicago, IL 60606, 312-922-5909)

Regents Credit Bank: One-stop evaluation

The Regents Credit Bank is a practical answer to the problem of "regularizing" college credit.

Many people have attended more than one college in their quest for an education. A major difficulty is that each time a person changes schools, a new evaluation of credits is required.

Each new school determines the worth of previous academic and nonacademic credits according to its own standards.

The problem becomes even more complicated in determining the number of credits that may be granted for foreign study, pass/fail courses, quarter hour/trimester credits conversions, correspondence study and informal learning experiences.

The University of the state of New York has established the Regents Credit Bank to end the confusion. It is an evaluation and transcript service for persons who want to consolidate their academic records.

For a fee of $450, anyone in the world can register for the Regents Credit Bank and have all college-level work records listed, provided they meet academic standards set by Regents College faculty members. Evaluations are given for a one-year period and results are placed on a master transcript. Each time a new course is submitted to the Bank, a report showing the total accumulation of academic credits to date is returned. Upon request, copies of this transcript will be sent to any institution for a $7 fee.

The Regents Credit Bank not only evaluates college-level work, but also all other prior learning, including nonacademic career and learning experiences, correspondence study, proficiency exams, foreign study, military educational experiences, independent study and special learning. People who have taken advantage of the Credit Bank Service are sometimes amazed to see how many credits they have accumulated over the years.

The Credit Bank does not evaluate a student's work toward the requirements for a particular degree, however—it's still up to a college or university to decide that. Nor is the Bank intended for those who enroll in the Regents College degree program with the University of the State of New York, because this service is automatically provided to those persons.

For more free information about the Regents Credit Bank Service contact the Regents Credit Bank, 1450 Western Avenue, Albany, NY 12203-3524 or call 518-474-3703.

The learning contract

Is time still the problem? You want to make progress toward a degree, but on your own terms and at your own pace?

Look into a learning contract.

A learning contract is an organized plan of study extending over a specific period of time to fulfill a particular aspect of a student's overall degree plan. This plan is formally agreed to by the student and the faculty adviser(s). The components of a learning contract typically include:

- *Focus:* description of study and learning objectives

- *Methods*: means the student will use to achieve objectives

- *Resources:* major resources to be used (e.g., library resources, field research, laboratory research, consultants, internships, studio work, course attendance), and the availability of these resources

- *Procedure:* specific activities to be employed to achieve objectives and credit to be awarded for successful completion of activities

- *Time estimate:* target date(s) for meeting specified objectives

- *Documentation:* evidence that the objectives have been fulfilled

- *Validation:* manner in which the evidence is to be evaluated

Learning contracts may be initiated by you or faculty members to satisfy specific course requirements or a block of study. There are no restrictions on the total number of credits you may earn. Credit awarded will vary considerably depending on the school and the complexity of the contract itself.

The learning contract has several advantages. Signing a contract commits you to work toward meeting specified learning objectives. A learning contract may be initiated and completed at any time during the year. You study at your own convenience and pace. You can decide whether to study traditional subjects in a traditional manner, or you might design an innovative program incorporating a variety of nontraditional study. The flexible nature of contract learning offers you full partnership in determining the content of the degree program, the study format, the materials to be used and how the work is to be evaluated.

Make an appointment with a college adviser in your area of study to explore the possibilities of a learning contract.

No-residency/Short-residency programs

Still, you might discover that your progress toward a degree or certificate isn't steady enough through correspondence study or some other arrangement. In other words, one course doesn't necessarily lead to another one. What you need is a step-by-step program of study, but without the hassle of commuting to a campus.

Imagine a university without walls: one that is practically everywhere you are.

There is an such an opportunity offered through the University Without Walls (UWW) Consortium, which is an international network of colleges and universities offering bachelor's, master's and doctoral programs through external study. These are not "diploma mills," but accredited institutions—some of them quite well-known—that specialize, among other things, in nontraditional study.

For instance, the first graduates of Mind Extension University did not attend class or meet with professors to earn their degrees. Instead, they were among the 36,000 people enrolled nationwide who tuned in to classes via cable TV. Glenn Jones, creator of the program and chairman and chief executive of Colorado's Jones Intercable Inc., said, "We make quality education available to everyone in the country regardless of their position in life and regardless of where they are."

Three fully accredited degree programs are offered through Mind Extension University, including a bachelor's in management from the University of Maryland's University College; a master of arts in education and human development from George Washington University; and a master of business administration from Colorado State.

Classes are taped at 21 colleges and universities and are cablecast free into cable-subscriber homes. Students enroll by calling a toll-free number and order books with credit cards. They communicate with professors by telephone or electronic mail, and they mail in assignments and independently proctored tests.

Mind Extension University's first four MBA graduates tuned in from Alaska, California, Connecticut and Oklahoma. One student who works as a systems analyst for the U.S. Postal Service noted, "The key was the flexibility, given that I have a family life that I needed to maintain."

Jones' vision is to "make all America a school to create excitement about education and to make it a lifelong process." For more information, call 800-727-5663.

A big difficulty eliminated by cable or satellite distance learning, as it's called, is residency requirements: these differ between institutions. Some colleges require that students spend only a day or two on campus to fulfill program residency requirements, while others require a few weeks on campus. Some colleges require occasional on-campus seminars or workshops; others may require completion of a minimum number of regular on-campus college hours.

On the other hand, you can complete an entire degree program at a reasonable cost, with absolutely no residency required at all, through American Open University, California State University/Dominguez Hills, Charter Oak College, City University, Embry-Riddle Aeronautical University, Empire State College, Indiana University, Ohio University, Regents College, Thomas Edison State College, University of Iowa, University of Missouri/Columbia, University of Nevada/Reno, Weber State University and other institutions. (See Appendix 3 for a complete list.)

Each college listed differs in cost, admission and program requirements. But with a few exceptions, all the colleges offer advanced placement by previously earned credits for academic study, life experience, equivalency and challenge examinations, military experience and other relevant learning experiences.

On-line education at home

Some of the research done for this chapter was done via computer: browsing information databases, magazine collections, even libraries—one of them at Oxford University in Britain!

Computer networking can bring you advice, counsel and news of important developments on the run, more than any ancient king or queen could ever have commanded.

It's tremendously empowering: You convene the best minds in education with a few keystrokes.

It's truly democratic: There's no one representing you; no credentialism is necessary. The doors of great institutions fly open when you knock.

It can be your magic carpet to college campuses all over the country. All you need to start beaming yourself hither and yon is a computer, a modem and some inexpensive software.

But first, before you start looking into computers and software, pick up a copy of one of these books and read a bit (maybe I should have said "read a byte"):

Crossing the Internet Threshold by Roy Tennant, John Oper and Anne G. Lipow, 1993. This instructional handbook, written by librarians, is designed to be used for learning and for further training. Provides both beginners' information and trainers' aids for all basic Internet functions. $45. Library Solutions Institute, 2137 Oregon Street, Berkeley, CA 94705. For information, send e-mail to ALIPOW@ LIBRARY.BERKELEY.EDU.

Internet Basics by Roy Tennant, 1992. This digest introduces the Internet computer network and provides an overview of the applications and resources the network provides. Specific topics include electronic mail, remote login (telnet), file transfer and extended services such as WAIS, Gopher and Archie. Free with SASE. Write ERIC Clearinghouse on Information Resources, 030 Huntington Hall, Syracuse University, Syracuse, NY 13244-2340; 315-443-3640.

Zen and the Art of the Internet, Second Edition by Brendan P. Kehoe, 1993. Aimed at the novice user, this book is intended to serve as a reference work and a foundation from which network users can explore the realm of Internet resources. $22. Prentice Hall, 200 Old Tappan Road, Old Tappan, NJ 07675; 800-922-0579.

The Whole Internet: User's Guide & Catalog by Ed Krol. A complete guide to the Internet, covering everything from the basics, like electronic mail and newsgroups, to the newest developments. O'Reilly & Associates, Inc., 103 Morris Street, Suite A, Sebastopol, CA 95472 (This book is available in many bookstores.)

Then you'll be ready to try tapping into resources like these:

ERIC/IR (ERIC Clearinghouse on Information Resources) is one of 16 clearinghouses in the ERIC System, which is sponsored by the Office of Educational Research and Improvement, U.S. Department of Education. ERIC/IR specializes in educational technology and library/information science and processes documents in these areas for the ERIC database. The clearinghouse also provides user services and publications related to its scope areas, including the ERIC Networker, electronic "help sheets" for using ERIC resources on the Internet. Write 030 Huntington Hall, Syracuse University, Syracuse, NY 13244-2340; 315-443-3640. Program contact: Nancy Preston.

Learning Link national consortium

Learning Link is a computer-based, interactive communication system for educators, students, adult learners and public television viewers. It features databases and information resources, message centers, and mail and gateways to remote sites. Its services are locally managed and operated by public broadcasting stations, education agencies or community organizations in 13 states. A national version is available to those who do not have access to the local version. The national consortium provides technical support and editorial content. Site operators tailor the services to meet community needs. WNET/13, 356 West 58th Street, New York, NY 10019; 212-560-6613.

Sound like wonderful opportunities? They are. And they're just waiting for you to *login*.

In Chapter 8, "How Will I Keep My Education Current?" there is more information about databases like CompuServe and NewsNet.

Community colleges: Three paths to success

And speaking of opportunities, right in your backyard are *three* educational opportunities rolled into one—the community college.

Not only do community colleges offer *two-year transfer degrees* that serve as the freshman and sophomore years of a four-year program, but they also make available *two-year associate degrees* and *certificate programs*, designed to make you job-ready right away.

Remember, at the beginning of this chapter it was pointed out that 60 percent of jobs don't require a four-year degree. A community college lets you examine the middle ground between a high school diploma and a bachelor's degree.

Certificate programs

For instance, if you want to be trained in a trade, such as heating and air conditioning maintenance, electrical repair, automotive repair, real estate appraising, plumbing or a host of other practical skills, then you don't need courses in political science, history and psychology. Nor do you want to spend the time in class that those courses require. Maybe what will suit your needs is a certificate program.

Certificate programs can last anywhere from four weeks to two years, depending on the required coursework. The majority of certificate programs are professionally oriented. Students pursue these programs to prepare for new careers, to qualify for a promotion, to stay current in their field, to satisfy mandated education requirements, or simply to acquire new skills and knowledge. For example, the emergence of computers in the business world ushered in a whole new specialization in computer repair, a popular program. Opportunities like this may not be available through two- or four-year university-sponsored degree programs.

Also, in many states, a certificate program is a prerequisite for both professional licensure and employment, especially in highly specialized fields such as real estate, insurance brokerage and the allied health professions. In some states, certificate programs are also mandated for relicensure purposes. People who work in these states are required to pursue certificate programs either by their professional association or by the state itself. The certificate does not, however, *guarantee* licensure, employment or promotion unless it has been mandated as the only prerequisite to advancement.

The curriculum typically includes a number of required courses and a few electives. Some programs also require a practicum or internship. Often, courses taken as part of a certificate program are applicable to degree programs at the college or university offering the certificate program.

Most certificate programs have admission requirements, which vary considerably from program to program. Some programs require applicants to hold particular educational credentials, take an entrance examination, submit transcripts and letters of reference and recommendation, and visit the program coordinator for an interview. Because entry requirements differ greatly, you should contact individual program administrators for information concerning specific admission requirements and program prerequisites.

Here are some typical certificate programs. (Ones that are part of an apprenticeship program—a cooperative agreement between organized labor and a college—are noted as such.)

Automobile mechanic
Biomedical equipment
    technician
Bricklayer (apprentice)
Cabinetmaker
Carpenter (apprentice)
Computer peripheral
    equipment
Computer programmer
Cosmetologist
Dental laboratory
    technician

Drafter, architectural
Drafter, mechanical
Electrical repairer (apprentice)
Electrician (apprentice)
Electronics technician
    (apprentice)
Fire fighter
Heating and air-conditioning
    installer (apprentice)
Legal secretary
Machinist (apprentice)
Medical laboratory technician

Realtor
Security guard
Sheet metal worker
(apprentice)

...anic

degree in applied science

...ate in applied science (AAS) degree is awarded to
...ho earn 60 hours of credit—about four semesters—in a
...sequence of courses. These degrees are for students who
...preparing for a career that requires study beyond high school,
...t does not require a four-year degree. AAS degrees have two
components: specialized courses in a major field of study—interior
design, for example—and general education courses such as
English and social science.

Generally an AAS degree can be completed in two years, but
many students work toward completion part-time.

Keep in mind that these two-year programs are *not* designed to
be the freshmen and sophomore years of a four-year degree: They
prepare a student for entry into the work force immediately. Here
are some examples of AAS degree programs:

Architectural drafting
technology
Aviation pilot training
Child development
Dental hygiene
Finance and credit
management
Fire science technology
Graphic communications

Industrial electrician
(apprentice)
Interior design
Management and supervision
Mechanical design
Office administration
Police science
Real estate
Teacher aide

Transfer or associate in arts degree

Finally, more and more students—recent high school graduates
and returning adults—are enrolling in community college transfer
degree programs. For students who want to "test the waters" of
college, or who want to save money on the first two years of
college, an associate in arts program fits the bill.

It focuses on the arts, humanities and social scien
ovides an excellent foundation for further study in such
rt, English, business, education, foreign language, histo
iberal arts, music, philosophy, political science, psychology,
ogy, social work, speech, theater and many other majors.
transfer to a four-year program at a college or university,
associate in arts degree will serve as your freshmen and sop
more years.

It's a good idea, however, to choose your transfer program wit.
the guidance of a community college adviser. Depending on the
field you plan to study for your bachelor's degree, the coursework
in the associate program will vary.

For instance, a typical associate program in science and math
might include courses in astronomy, biology, geology, chemistry,
math, physical science, physics and zoology. In social science, the
program might require courses in anthropology, economics, geo-
graphy, history, political science, psychology, social science and
sociology.

An added benefit to approaching a four-year degree from this
direction is this: If your high school grades were modest or poor, a
college or university will put much more emphasis on your work at
a community college. In other words, you can give yourself more
time to get the credentials you need to enroll in a selective four-
year program.

Should you consider a private career school?

You seen the ads on television: "Become a professional by receiving a state-of-the-art education in one of today's hottest career
fields." The field might be computer repair, allied health or
business. The school is private.

Since World War II, the growth of private career schools has
been closely related to changes in federal student aid policy. Starting with the Veterans Education Benefits program after World
War II, and continuing to today's student aid program, proprietary
school students have used government student grants and loans.
The 1972 Amendments to the Higher Education Act provided full
and equal participation with traditional higher education students.

But private career schools differ from traditional higher education in several important ways.

First, many offer programs lasting less than a year and do not grant degrees, although nearly 300 private career schools—a sizable exception—offer at least an associate degree.

Second, private career schools are businesses: Their goal is to make a profit for private owners. Proprietary schools, as they're called by educators, have placed decision-making in the hands of the owner, with no tradition of faculty senate or collegial decision making. Teaching positions are less permanent, because instructors have no tenure. However, on the positive side, private career schools tend to be more sensitive to market forces than traditional colleges. They can shift quickly to meet the needs of employers and the interests of students.

What all this means to you is, first, a private career school will probably ask you to sign a contract. Second, the classes will be more expensive than at the local community college. But, third, there will be a strongly practical bent to the education.

Private career schools offer literally hundreds of programs. The majority of students enroll in office, technology and personal service programs. The technical areas are dominated by auto mechanics and computer-related fields, but courses of study run the gamut from broadcast technology to architectural engineering.

Those classes are more structured and oriented toward job skills than usually found in traditional colleges. All students in a program generally take the same sequence of courses, with a new class starting as quickly as every two or three weeks. Much more hands-on education is available, with less emphasis on theory than in the collegiate sector.

About 60 percent of the students enrolling in private career schools receive a certificate or degree, compared to just over 40 percent for students in community colleges (although some community college students never intend to receive a certificate or a degree).

In the short run, earnings of proprietary school graduates are similar to graduates from community college vocational programs. But little information is available about the longer-term effects on income of attending a private career school. Graduates report a high degree of satisfaction with their education, but a higher proportion of previously enrolled students report dissatisfaction with their education, compared with traditional college students. They are also more likely to report periods of unemployment than students attending other types of schools.

So before you enroll in a private career school, ask these questions:

- Will I be required to sign a contract?

- What happens if I don't complete the coursework—will I be liable for the balance of the tuition?

- What's the length of the program I'm interested in?

- Does the school offer career counseling and placement?

- What percentage of graduates receive jobs in their field?

- How long after graduation till they find a position?

- What are the names of employers who hire the school's graduates?

Take a tour of the school and talk with students who are presently enrolled—they'll give you the inside scoop.

And speaking of good information, the resources in Appendix 3 at th end of this book will put you directly in touch with many of the opportunities that were described in this one.

Interview
Get rid of your television set

According to Tom Roach, professor of communications at Purdue University, the odds against him attending college were phenomenal.

"I was in trouble a lot in high school because I had long hair and pulled pranks," Roach said. "I got suspended a lot."

In fact, when he asked to enroll in foreign language classes at his high school because his brother told him he should prepare for college, Roach's request was denied. His adviser said the classes were reserved for those who were likely to attend college.

Roach eventually dropped out of high school and went on to earn his GED. He said the only reason he decided to go to college was because of an interest in poetry and the lyrics of rock music.

"I was more interested in rock music, but it became an interest in poetry," Roach said. "For me, going to English classes was like going to rock concerts."

Roach entered Joliet Junior College at 21 years of age and graduated with an associate degree in journalism. He then went on to earn a BA in journalism and English and an MA in English from Northern Illinois University.

Roach never believed he would get very far in college, so he never imagined he would go on, later in life, to earn his Ph.D. from Northwestern University. After all, he was a high school dropout.

"None of my great career moves were anything I'd planned," Roach said. "I made the initiative to do these things, but the things that had to fall into place for me to get where I am—the odds for them happening were astronomical."

When Roach returned to college for his Ph.D., he was 37 years old. By that time he was married, had three small children and taught college courses in communications and public relations at Purdue.

Juggling work and school

Roach began his work at Purdue as a visiting professor, pending completion of his Ph.D. To be tenure track, he needed the degree.

Although other professors advised him to keep student inter- action down and reuse his class syllabi so he could concentrate on his degree, Roach, a highly interactive teacher, couldn't follow this advice.

"I just made arrangements with Purdue to keep my workload down until I finished my degree," Roach said. "I limited my teach- ing to no more than three days a week."

Juggling a family and school

Handling family demands and higher education simultaneously presented a greater challenge to Roach. He had three children, the oldest one under 6 years old.

"I compensated for not being home by taking my children with me," Roach said. "This wasn't always easy."

Roach described one week when he was taking comprehensive exams at the University, teaching at Purdue and running a sheriff's campaign. His wife, Sue, was in the hospital that week and all three of his children got the flu.

"I had to bring my kids with me to take my exams at Northwestern and teach at Purdue," Roach said. "Between classes we went to my office and I hoped one of the kids wouldn't vomit."

"At night I dropped the kids off with my mom and visited Sue in the hospital," Roach continued. "It was one of the most intense weeks of my life, but we won the election, and I passed my comps."

Roach said he and his wife both had to make sacrifices to compensate for his hectic schedule.

"We were involved in a lot of projects, like rehabbing the house and other community-oriented activities," Roach said. "We had to scale back."

"Sue made some major sacrifices for me," Roach continued. "She sat up until two in the morning editing papers and sometimes drove me places she didn't want to be because I was too tired."

Roach said his wife never questioned whether he should return to college. "She was extraordinarily supportive," he said.

Time management

Roach's method of dealing with the various demands in his life was quite atypical. He didn't write out a schedule or plan his time but simply prioritized the things he had to do to make sure they would get done.

"I always knew when there was something I had to do," Roach said. "When that time came I dropped what I was involved in and did it. I tried to remain as spontaneous as possible. That's just the opposite of what most people would do."

Advice for beginning adult college students

Roach graduated from Northwestern University in spring of 1994 with a Ph.D. in communication studies/rhetorical inquiry. He offered the following advice to potential college students:

- "Stick to it. You can't succeed unless you take the risk."
- "Oh, and get rid of your television set."

Chapter 3

How Do I Get Started On My Plans?

Let's say you're starting from scratch—you want to make progress toward some educational goal, but you're not sure where to begin.

In this chapter, you'll learn step-by-step how to uncover your options. Just follow along, and then I'll explain how to assemble the credentials you'll need for admissions to various types of programs.

Step 1: Locate opportunities

You may already have spent some time rummaging through the reference section of your local library looking up addresses and taking notes on schools, apprenticeships, and so on. Actually, you have an easy-to-use directory of all sorts of opportunities right in your home: the yellow pages.

Open up to the heading "Schools." In my yellow pages I have three pages of addresses and phone numbers, from the Acme School of Bartending ("state approved—free brochure") to Tyler School of Secretarial Sciences. In between are three community colleges; two universities, seven travel schools; two truck driving schools; 10 beauty schools; a school of court reporting; a school of heating and refrigeration repair; and 38 public and private schools—grades kindergarten through high school.

What should I do? Easy—I should start calling and requesting information: a list of course offerings; a schedule of classes; a guarantee of having met state standards; a schedule of fees; and a description of the facilities.

You might think at first that this is overkill: requesting all kinds of printed information from hither and yon. But at this point, you're just shopping. Okay, so you don't plan to go to travel school; but you always have been curious about how much training travel agents have, and how they learn their trade. So why not? Take a peek at that type of school.

On the other hand, maybe you're already pretty focused: you know you want a degree in speech pathology. Whoa! This is not a common program of study. You can put down your telephone directory at this point.

And pick up instead a copy of the *Index to Majors* (College Board). It lists programs of study in alphabetical order and the institutions that offer them, state-by-state. Many libraries carry it and quite a few high school guidance centers, too.

Which brings up an important point...

You don't need to undertake your exploration of educational options by yourself. You are living in a community college or high school district, even if you live in an unincorporated area. There are experts in those publicly funded buildings, and you have a right to avail yourself of their time and advice.

I'm the coordinator of the guidance department in a high school of 2,100 students. And I receive telephone calls weekly, at least, from residents and even persons who live out-of-district seeking information about financial aid and programs of study. A routine phone call for instance is a request from a former student for his or her high school transcript. Sometimes these callers have been out of school for 20 years or more.

So if you want to take the shortcut to your goal, first do a reasonable amount of research on your own; then make an appointment with a high school guidance counselor or a career counselor at a community college and find out what you need to know.

Here are some other sources of information, too:

The local library. This might seem obvious, but many people overlook three resources I strongly recommend. The first is the reference librarian. It's not too "cheeky" of you just to walk up and say, "I'm looking into taking classes—do you have some information on that?" This exactly the type of "Please help me, I'm lost" type of question that send most reference librarians into their favorite role: rescuing the confused patron.

You might be directed to the pamphlet file, filled with articles and fliers and booklets organized under headings like "Schools," "Education," "Studying" and so on. You might be shown how to do a computerized search of hundreds of magazines in the library's collection using a system like Infotrac or Academic Abstracts. It's easy—just type the name of a topic like "adult education" and let the software do the rest. A high school student in the magazine room will even pull the issues of publications on your printout. Finally, your reference librarian will also have freebies on hand like copies of the local park district bulletin—always a possibility for interesting classes—or bulletins about special opportunities like income tax seminars; guest speakers at local chuches and temples; and programs at the library itself.

Oh, yes! Libraries are much more now than places where people go "Shhhh!" around old books. Many libraries have auditoriums, or at least meeting rooms, where anyone is invited to hear speakers on topics like genealogy, gardening, quilting, ham radios, and many other hobbies. Or participate in discussions about popular books, classic works, political events, matters of local concern—you name it.

All you need to do is attend.

The personnel office at work. Some personnel offices are still the type that feature drab green walls and long tables for filling out applications. But many have transformed themselves in true human resources centers that resemble career counseling offices. Information is available about personal and professional development: where to enroll in executive training classes; when to sign-up for an exam that can lead to a promotion, and so on. Make an appointment with the director and outline your general goals. Here's a tip: some businesses will subsidize their employees' education. In other words, your company might pay for your tuition if the course(s) are job-related. Check it out.

The church or temple. I know a number of people who have attended retreats or classes organized by their place of worship, and many times the insights they've gained have enriched their lives. You see, it's one thing to read a book about reaching your life goals, and quite another to spend a weekend with other adults who are searching, too. In fact, the questions you're struggling with might not be the type that a typical lecture or class can answer: you need to explore a more personal dimension. Look into the opportunities a priest, minister, or rabbi can offer you and your family.

Step 2: Organize your information

If you've always depended on posting flyers, letters, permission slips, and outstanding bills on the refrigerator door, you'll have to change your method of organization if you want to get the most of your educational plans.

It's not that being back in school as an adult is more complicated, but think of it this way: as you make phone calls to various persons at libraries or park districts—registrars, admissions counselors, faculty members, etc.—you're going to be receiving key details about deadlines, addresses, class times, and so on.

Don't make your planning more difficult that it has to be. Get a notebook for those times when someone you're talking to says, "Here's what you need—can you take this down?"

Second, use a calendar. If you're like a lot of adults, you have plenty of commitments as it is: kid's baseball games, school committee meetings, and the rest. To make an informed decision about when and where to enroll in classes, you need to see the big picture—available time versus reserved time. Don't frustrate yourself by creating conflicts that can avoided with a little creative time management (see Chapter 5, How Will I Juggle Family, Work and School?, for more details on this).

Third, reserve a special drawer in your desk or file cabinet for printed information, applications, and correspondence, for example—all the things connected with your educational plans. You'll see immediately how this will benefit you. Let's say, for instance, you have an appointment with an admissions counselor. If your educational credentials are in a file of their own, you can grab it and be confident you have what you need.

And speaking of educational credentials, which ones will you need, and how do you get copies of already existing ones?

Step 3: Gather together and organize your records

For a teacher or adviser to assist you with your plans, it's important that you provide certain, official information about the educational experiences you've already had.

Some or all of the records described next might be required for admission to some programs.

Your high school transcript

Realize, to start with, you don't need to be a high school graduate to enter certain college programs. If you did finish high school, however, colleges usually require a certified high school record. This record of all courses and grades is called a transcript.

You can get an official copy of your transcript by writing to the high school from which you graduated (or its school district office); identifying yourself and your high school and years of attendance and graduation (even if you graduated as long as 40 or 50 years earlier, your records are still there!); and requesting that a copy of your transcript be sent to the college's admissions office. To be acceptable to admissions offices, transcripts must be sent directly from the school to the college.

Make the request for your high school transcript at least six to eight weeks before a college's deadline. And remember that the high school may be completely closed from mid-June to mid-September. Also, the high school might charge a small fee for providing the transcript.

If you earned a high school equivalency diploma (GED), have the adult education program—or other agency that awarded the equivalency diploma—send a transcript of your records to the college admissions offices.

If your high school records have somehow been destroyed through fire or other accident, ask the college admissions offices for instructions on how to proceed. Affidavits of specified kinds attesting to your high school graduation may be accepted.

Even without a high school diploma, some colleges permit an applicant to take courses on a trial basis. Such coursework should be fully acceptable in the study program leading to the degree you want.

As an alternative, you could study for and take tests to earn a General Equivalency Diploma (see Chapter 2). Preparatory classes and testing for a GED are regularly offered by public high school systems and community colleges. You can find out the details by writing or telephoning the office of the superintendent of schools of your community public school system. The information is probably also available in a public library.

College transcripts

Transcripts of previous college studies you've completed are also often required for admission. You can request these in the same way you did your high school transcript.

Your college transcript is valuable to you. It can be used to award "transfer credit" toward your degree, if your previous coursework is applicable in content and difficulty level.

Transcripts of your college-level work are available from an institution's office of admissions and records. Call the general information number of the campus and ask to be transferred. Have ready the dates you attended classes, and your social security number. Finally, have the exact address you want the transcript sent to, as well.

There might be a small fee—say, $5. Don't try to save yourself the cost by making a photocopy of your transcripts or report cards yourself and mailing them off. Nearly all programs of post-high school study—apprenticeships, certificate programs, graduate schools—require official copies of educational records. Have them sent directly from the institution you attended.

Test scores

Most college programs designed especially for adults have no test requirements. For others, though, you might have to take an entrance test. With adult students, colleges often use test results for guidance and placement rather than for admissions acceptance or rejection. Individual colleges set their own requirements.

The entrance tests most often required for undergraduate admission are the Scholastic Aptitude Test (SAT) of the College Board and the American College Testing Program Assessment (ACT). A number of colleges accept the results of either the SAT or ACT. Some colleges require other tests such as the Achievement Tests of the College Board, which are tests in specific high school subjects (like chemistry, French or American history). If any of those are required, a college's admission office will tell you.

Information about the tests—test registration, fees, and testing sites—is available from:

The College Board	ACT Registration
Admissions Testing Program	Box 414
Box 592	Iowa City, IA 52234
Princeton, NJ 08541	

Study materials with which to prepare for these tests are provided in the bulletins and other literature sent when you register. See the test review books listed under "Tests" in Appendix 3.

Recommendation letters

Colleges often require a secondary school recommendation for high school-age graduates. If the college you're applying to requires a high school recommendation, request one at the same time you write for your high school transcript. Understandably, you may no longer have any personal contacts at the school, so ask whether the guidance department can write a recommendation based on your transcript, using your grades and coursework to predict your capability for college level work. In a separate letter of your own, add information about your work life or courses you have taken that are relevant.

If other recommendation letters are required, request them from present or former teachers, from supervisors at work or professionals who have some acquaintance with your abilities. Ask for these evaluations long before the college's deadline so the writers have enough time. Supply them with already addressed envelopes. It's a good idea to send a thank-you note, too.

Replying to offers of admission/financial aid

Several weeks or even months may go by before you start to receive decisions on your admissions and financial aid applications.

If you've applied to more than one college, wait until you've heard from all the colleges before deciding which offer to accept. *Always wait until you've heard from all the financial aid offices— offers will differ.* (See Chapter 4 for much more information about financial aid.) If a college seems to be pressing you for a reply, either try to get an extension or ask for decisions on your other applications.

Once you have considered your options and made your final choice, reply by the deadline—May 1, in most cases. Be sure to respond to any other acceptances you receive, declining their offers and expressing your thanks. This sort of courtesy is a good policy, and might even have some practical value to you later.

At last! You the student

Congratulations! You've been accepted as a student in the college you applied to. You are now, officially, back in school.

You might feel a little anxious, however—adult students often do. That's understandable. But you needn't worry about getting started, because the rest of this chapter will guide you through the key activities of registering for courses, getting the most out of your classes and sharpening those abilities you'll need to succeed.

To actually start being a student, it's not necessary to wait until the first day of registration, however. The first step is to get some good advice specific to your interests and goals. Here's how:

Meet with your adviser

You'll probably be assigned an adviser by the school. But if you're not, or the adviser seems uninterested or uninformed—some are graduate students who have been on campus for a year or less, unfortunately—look for another. There are at least four other persons to seek advice from: a counselor in the admissions office; the head of the program you've chosen; the chairperson of your department; or a faculty member in your field. Asking a department secretary for the names of a few senior students in your program isn't a bad idea, either. Call them and ask for do's and don'ts. After all, they are right where you'll be in a few years.

Spend time reading the course catalog

The course catalog is the owner's manual of the college or university. Read it at least several days before the scheduled opening of your registration period for the term. In it, or in accompanying bulletins, you'll find:

- Official course numbers and names

- Brief summaries of course content

- Credit value of the course

- When and where particular classes meet

- Prerequisite courses (required or recommended to be taken before enrolling in the course being described)

- Name of the instructor

Typically, catalogs outline course combinations recommended for students in each level of a program: what you should take first semester, second semester, and so on. Build your first-term schedule around your program's introductory courses and basic requirements. Resist the temptation to plunge into high-level courses, even if they sound fascinating. It's not that you can't handle them, but they might not fit your program of study. Elective courses will allow you to explore a little: choose these with the help of an adviser.

Now, keep in mind that it's unlikely you'll get exactly the courses you want at exactly the right times. Consequently, be prepared to go to registration with two or three drafts of a course schedule in hand (the advantage to being a beginning student is that you can choose from a wide range of courses in your program). Decide which courses you might add or drop from your draft schedules, just in case.

Registration

All right, prepare for blast-off. Registration is the first major activity following your admission to a program of study. It's also the time that you may have to make last-minute decisions about adding or dropping courses—or instructors—and it's also the time you pay tuition and fees for the coming term.

Here are some tips on completing the "registration maze," which has improved considerably with the use of computers. In fact, you might even be able to register from a touch-tone phone. In addition, many colleges offer enrolled students the opportunity to preregister. You submit your course request forms for the coming term before the close of your current term. But should you have to go through a traditional stand-in-line type registration process, then:

- Prepare for delays: Estimate how much time you think you'll need to register and then double it.

- Bring your course catalog, drafts of schedules, identification and checkbook.

- Go to the designated location at the earliest time you can manage: on the very first day or night of the registration period. By going early you can avoid being closed out of desired courses and sections because of full enrollment.

- Rest assured that what seems to be final may not in fact be final. In other words, there is usually a period running for several days after registration in which changes in courses and class sessions can be made without penalty. If a class doesn't pan out because your circumstances change, there is even a specified time *after* the opening of classes during which students can drop courses for which they have registered, with full or partial refunds of their tuition payments. But watch your deadlines!

Your student ID card

You'll be issued a student ID card, which might seem redundant because your driver's license looks very similar. However, a student ID card is your passport to the campus library, special presentations, even reductions in book and activity fees in some cases. So carry your ID with you. Don't make the mistake of not getting one until you absolutely have to have it. The office that issues them might be closed at that time.

Your textbooks

Campus bookstores have lists of the textbooks and supplies required for classes—just have your course number(s) handy. Get your textbooks as soon as you can, so you'll have them at the beginning of class. Inventories sometimes sell out early in a term. By delaying, you may have to wait until a new shipment arrives. On the other hand, a college's own bookstore or other nearby bookstores may offer used textbooks at about half the price of new copies. This strategy saves money, but be sure your books are the editions specified for your course and not previous editions.

Starting your coursework

Once you've registered, it's time to get down to business. Start by outfitting yourself with basic learning tools that include the following:

- A standard desk dictionary, preferably the latest edition. Ask a teacher or librarian to recommend one if you're unsure which to choose.

- A manual of correct English usage. A classic is *The Elements of Style* by William Strunk, Jr. and E.B. White, available in the reference section of most bookstores. A new book I find very useful is *Plain Style: Techniques for Simple, Concise, Emphatic Business Writing* by Richard Lauchman. (American Management Association, 1993. $15.95.) If you're taking a required introductory course in English composition, wait to see which reference is recommended for the course.

- A pocket calculator or even a computer can be an essential tool for programs heavy in mathematics, science or technology. You might wait to see what types are recommended for use in the specific program you're taking. Moreover, the college may make preferred calculators or computers available at substantial discounts.

- Notebooks, pens and a bookbag, backpack or briefcase.

The first session in each of your courses will be especially interesting, for you'll be meeting the person who teaches the course and learning essentially what the course will be like. Follow these basic steps at your first class meetings:

- Make a list of the required texts or other books to get.

- Note any special supplies or equipment that may be needed or recommended.

- If appropriate, get a reading list for the course that identifies all required textbooks and supplementary reading sources. The reading list may include the dates by which to complete specified readings.

- Get a copy of the syllabus or outline of topics covered in the course, or make notes on the instructor's verbal description of course content and coverage.

- Note the instructor's policies concerning attendance requirements; class participation; amount and kinds of outside assignments; numbers, kinds and timing of term papers and exams; and basis for grading.

- Make a record of office hours when the instructor is available to answer questions or help clear up difficulties you may be having with the course.

- Ask questions about any aspect of the course that isn't clear to you, either during or after the class session.

So now you're on the starting line of being a student. You're enrolled, you're eager, you're making progress.

There's just one more important consideration: paying for all this.

Don't worry—that's the next chapter.

Chapter 4

How Do I Pay for More Education?

Education after high school isn't cheap. When you add up the cost of tuition, books, transportation—maybe even room and board, if you want to live on campus—it can be a considerable investment.

Investment is the right word, however. Studies show that the lifetime earning power of someone with post-high school training or education far exceeds that of worker with a high school diploma only. Does $750,000 more in your pocket over 30 years sound appealing? That's an often-used estimate of the difference.

So before you tremble over newspaper stories about four years of college costing as much as your house, remember: The payback is practically guaranteed. And financial aid is your ace-in-the-hole.

"Financial aid?" you're thinking—"I already make a good buck and my debts are small. I'm not going to qualify."

Listen, financial aid is not just for applicants strapped for money. It's to help anyone meet the costs of post-high school education. In the federal and state financial aid system, there's a formula based on your age, income, savings, number of children, number of family members in college—and a handful of other factors—which is used to determine your eligibility. Some applicants who earn $100,000 a year qualify for aid; some who make $21,000 a year do not. It depends on what you're able to contribute.

In addition, there are lots of private funds available, too. These might be offered by organizations, businesses, associations or colleges themselves.

But you have to file a financial aid form to get in the running. More and more, even local civic groups offering money require scholarship candidates to submit a copy of their financial aid form.

And here's one more very important reason for filing for aid: if your income should change drastically while you're in school—say, because your spouse loses his or her job, or, worse, there's a death in the family—campus financial aid offices maintain a fund of emergency money *for students who are in the financial aid system.* If you have a form on file, you're okay; if not, well...

Now, you may have already received unsolicited mail saying that "millions of dollars in financial aid go unclaimed every year!" and the sender is offering to do a financial aid search for you. Or a postcard might announce, WE HAVE $2,000 IN YOUR NAME AVAILABLE. PLEASE ADVISE.

All right, here's some free advice:

The reason millions goes unclaimed in financial aid every year is that some scholarships have stipulations so narrow, practically no one qualifies for the money. For example, when I was in the admissions office at the University of Chicago, we offered a scholarship earmarked by the donor for any enrolling student who hailed from a town with the word "Smith" in it: Smithson, Smithton, Smithberg—you name it. As you can imagine, some years no one from Smith-anywhere showed up. The money went unclaimed.

Second, you can do a financial aid search yourself and save $45 to $75, whatever the service is charging. It takes some legwork, but realize that nearly all private search companies guarantee finding a minimum of five sources of aid. Sure, it sounds good, but three—if not more—will probably be tied to military service. Don't complain—the armed services offers plenty of financial aid for college: Just raise your right hand, please. With some effort, you can find at least five *useful* sources of financial aid you're eligible for.

And last, that windfall of $2,000 you're being offered out of the blue is a student loan, that's all. The service qualifies you for state or federal aid, and lends you borrowed money at a percentage point or two of interest above what you could get yourself, if you went to your local bank.

So let's get down to the business of finding money for your education, on your own, step-by-step.

First, assess your particular needs and preferences; establish your basic qualifications as a potential recipient by defining your educational and financial needs and goals. To help you do this, here are some general questions to ask yourself:

- What kinds of colleges or universities interest me?

- What careers or fields of study interest me?

- Do I plan to earn a degree?

- Am I only interested in financial aid that is a gift, or am I willing to consider a loan or exchanging work for assistance?

- In what parts of the country am I willing to live and study?

Second, consider any special circumstances or conditions that might qualify you for aid targeted for special audiences. Examine this area carefully, and remember that even slight or unlikely connections may be worth checking out. The most common qualifications and, oppositely, restrictions involve:

- gender
- race or ethnic group
- place of residence
- citizenship
- membership in an organization, such as a union, association, or fraternal group
- religious affiliation
- military or veteran status

- financial need
- merit or academic achievement
- creative or professional accomplishment

Some of these qualifiers may apply to the applicant as well as his or her parents, stepparents, guardians or spouse. If your parents are divorced, you should be aware of both parents' affiliations, even if you don't live with one or either of them. Likewise, even if your parents are deceased, you may be eligible for some awards based on their one-time status or affiliations. Or, given enough lead time, it might even be possible for you (or your parents) to join certain organizations, or establish residence, in time for you to be eligible for certain funds.

Third, start your financial aid search as soon as possible. Think about this: Certain scholarships that are granted by civic organizations—such as the Jaycees or Rotary—may require membership or a period of service to the community. By the time you're trying to make decisions about college, for example, it may be too late to meet the requirements. So to be safe, try to start your financial hunt as early as two years before you think you will need aid. If you allow enough time to complete all the necessary steps, you'll be more likely to identify, qualify for and meet application deadlines for a wide variety of awards. This will increase your chances of obtaining aid. Allow plenty of time to:

- Write for official applications. You won't be considered for some awards unless you apply using the correct forms.
- Read all instructions carefully.
- Take note of application deadlines, which aren't always in the fall of the school year.
- Accurately and completely file all required supporting material, such as essays and resumes. If you fail to answer certain questions, you may be disqualified even though you are a worthy candidate.
- Give references enough time to submit their recommendations: supervisors, colleagues and instructors, for instance.

Teachers, in particular, get many requests for letters of recommendation and should be given as much advance warning as possible.

Don't worry, though, if college is fast approaching or if you've already enrolled. Along with widely varying eligibility criteria, many awards have application deadlines that come up throughout the year. Keep looking, and you're sure to find some for which you qualify and may yet apply.

In fact, the next step is contacting colleges, universities and other educational institutions themselves. Most offer their own institution-specific financial aid programs. Their financial aid offices may also provide information on privately sponsored awards that are specifically designated for students of those institutions. Contact the financial aid office of any institution in which you have an interest and request applications and detailed information on all the aid programs they sponsor or administer.

Finally, make sure you plunder obvious resources for information about financial aid. On the federal level, contact the U.S. Department of Education at 400 Maryland Ave. SW, Washington, D.C. 20202, for up-to-date information on U.S. government award programs. Similarly, you should contact your state department of education for details on what is offered in your particular state.

There are also local sources of awards. A surprisingly large number of financial aid programs are sponsored by small or local organizations. Ask the reference librarian at your local library for help, or call your local chamber of commerce.

In addition, high school guidance counselors are often aware of local programs, and they can usually tell you how to get in touch with the sponsoring or administering organizations. Some high school guidance departments maintain files of local scholarships.

Local newspapers are also rich sources of information on financial aid programs. Start keeping a clip file.

Your library has a reference section: In it are financial aid directories, guides to paying for college and information about grants, scholarships and loans. Once again, ask your librarian for help.

Where the big money is

In counseling people about financial aid, I never discourage them from seeking out individual grants and scholarships. But I always mention that the big money comes from the colleges, universities and trade/technical schools themselves. In fact, 90 percent of the help students receive for paying for post-high school is campus-based money.

Both the federal and state governments have for many years provided important sources of financial aid to help qualified students. While the total amount of federal money available is subject to change based on funding levels, there is a commitment in Congress to a strong federal aid program. In addition, states and colleges and trade/technical schools provide aid for students through their own resources, and there are many other kinds of aid, need-based and otherwise, available through other programs. Notable among these are scholarships awarded by corporations, the military (through ROTC and service academy appointments) and athletic grants-in-aid.

The five major student financial aid programs, through which the majority of students requiring financial assistance receive aid, are administered by the federal government through the Department of Education. Two are grant programs—the Pell Grant and the Supplemental Educational Opportunity Grant (SEOG). Others are loan programs—the Perkins Loan and the Stafford Student Loan and its subsidiary loans, the PLUS for parents and the Supplemental Loans for Students (SLS). The fifth is College Work-Study (CWS), a program that helps colleges provide jobs for students on financial aid. Grants are outright gift awards and do not have to be repaid. Loans do have to be repaid, but at low interest (Perkins), moderate interest (Stafford), or market rates (PLUS and SLS) over a period of years.

Students apply directly for aid from the two largest programs, to the federal government for the Pell Grant and to a commercial bank for the Stafford Student Loan (including PLUS and SLS). Both Pell Grants and Stafford Student Loans are paid to the college the recipient is attending. These funds must be used to pay educational costs.

In contrast, funds for the other three programs—SEOG, Perkins, and CWS—are allocated among colleges for distribution to qualified students. In other words, students apply to the colleges, not to the government or to a bank, for these awards. College financial aid officers select the recipients of these moneys, usually creating a financial aid package for each eligible student that combines this campus-based aid with other federal assistance, such as Pell Grants and Stafford Student Loans, as well as with other forms of aid from the state, private organizations or the college itself.

To be eligible for any of the five federal programs, you have to meet clearly defined requirements:

- You must, for most programs, be enrolled at least half-time at an approved college or program of study (a limited number of students studying less than half-time may receive CWS awards and SEOG).

- You must be a U.S. citizen or a permanent resident.

- You must be an undergraduate (except for the loan and work-study programs, which are open to graduate students as well).

- You must use the assistance for educational expenses.

- You must not be in default on another student loan or owe a refund on a federal grant.

- You must qualify on the basis of need.

The only exceptions to the need requirement are PLUS and SLS. These loans do not require demonstration of need because they are intended to help families with higher incomes alleviate problems of "cash flow" rather than to meet established need.

Descriptions of these federal programs and the current amounts of each award are given in this chapter, along with information about how to determine eligibility and how to apply. All programs are subject to change, however, and students should check with a college financial aid officer for more information.

Pell Grant

The Pell Grant is the largest federal grant program, an estimated 3.5 million students receive awards annually. This grant is intended to be the base, or starting point, of assistance for lower-income families. Eligibility for a Pell Grant depends on a calculation of how much of a family's income and assets can go toward college costs.

The stipulated deadline to apply for a Pell Grant for the academic year is actually not until May 1. In other words, after a student is already in college. This is because the Pell program is an entitlement program, which means that everyone who needs a Pell Grant is supposed to get one. In reality, however, the funds could run out. So don't wait until the deadline.

Apply for a Pell Grant well before the start of the school year, when you apply for college and other forms of financial aid. (Most colleges require you to do this as part of your college aid application.) In response to you application you will receive a Student Aid Report (SAR), which will tell you whether you qualify for an award. If you have questions, you may call the Federal Student Aid Information Center: 800-4-FED-AID.

Supplemental Educational Opportunity Grant (SEOG)

This grant, as its name implies, is designed to provide additional need-based federal grant money to supplement the Pell Grant. A certain amount of money is given to each participating college to be awarded to especially needy students at the discretion of the financial aid office. Awards can range up to $4,000, the actual amount depending on financial need, the availability of SEOG funds at the college and the amount of other aid a student is receiving.

Application for this grant is not made directly. Rather, when you file for financial aid, you will automatically be in contention for these awards if you qualify. The filing date is the financial aid deadline established by the college. You will be told whether you are eligible for an SEOG when you receive financial aid notification from the college.

Perkins Loan

The Perkins Loan is a low-interest (currently 5 percent) loan for students with demonstrated need. These loans are assigned by the college financial aid office as part of a student's award package. You may borrow up to $4,500 during your first two years of college or a total of $9,000 for a complete undergraduate program of study ($18,000 is the limit for undergraduate plus graduate study). You may take up to 10 years to repay the loan, beginning nine months after you graduate, leave school or drop below half-time status. The repayment obligation is about 10 percent per month for each $1,000 borrowed. As with SEOG, you are automatically considered for this form of assistance when you apply for aid.

Stafford Student Loan, PLUS, and Supplemental Loans for Students

A Stafford Student Loan may be borrowed from a participating commercial lender, such as a bank, credit union, or savings and loan association. Some colleges are also approved lenders. The interest rate, backed by the federal government, is 8 percent. For you to be eligible to receive a Stafford Student Loan, you must demonstrate financial need.

The maximum amount of a Stafford Student Loan is $2,625 for each of the first two years, then up to $4,000 for each of three additional years for undergraduates. There is a $17,250 limit for your total undergraduate program ($54,750 is the ceiling for both undergraduate and graduate study). The lender normally allows 10 years for you to repay the loan. Your payments become due six months after your student status ends. The repayment is about 12 percent per month for each $1,000 borrowed for the first four years of repayment and then goes to 13 percent per month for each $1,000 borrowed (an increase in the interest rate from 8 percent to 10 percent) for the remainder of your obligation. However, 5 percent (or $125) is deducted from the amount of the loan and you receive $2,375. In addition, an insurance fee of about 1 percent may be deducted.

Application for a Stafford Student Loan, for which your college financial aid office has indicated you are eligible, should be made on a special Stafford Student Loan application form. This form will be sent to you or one can be picked up at a bank in your community. If you are unable to find a bank that participates in the program, contact your state department of education. Once you have found a lender, you fill out your part of the Stafford Student Loan application, the college then completes its section and returns the form to you, and you give it to the lender, which disburses the amount of the loan to the college.

The PLUS loan, part of the overall Stafford Student Loan program, is primarily for parents of dependent students. The same loan for independent undergraduate and graduate students is called SLS. These loans are not related to financial need but are intended to help remedy the "cash flow" problems that may occur when families or independent students are faced with paying college bills out of annual income. As with Stafford Student Loans, these two loans, which have a floating interest rate (now 9.3 percent), are made by lenders such as banks, savings and loan associations and some colleges.

There is a limit of $4,000 per year on PLUS and SLS, and the maximum amount that can be borrowed to help pay for undergraduate and graduate education is $20,000. It is important to note that, unlike Perkins and Stafford Student loans, for which repayment is deferred until after graduation, the repayment of PLUS and SLS loans begins 60 days after the money is advanced to the borrower, while the student is in college. There is a 10-year repayment period. At the current interest rate of 9.3 percent, the repayment obligation is about $12.65 per month for each $1,000 borrowed. There is, however, a $52 per-month minimum repayment obligation.

Application procedures are similar to those for the Stafford Student Loan. You should first try to find a bank in your community that participates in the PLUS/SLS program. Should you encounter difficulty in finding an eligible lender, contact your state department of higher education.

NOTE: Most federally funded loans are repayable beginning after graduation, or shortly after you drop out or stop taking classes. This means if you decide to take a semester or a year off, you must contact the lender and ask to extend the loan. Otherwise, you'll receive notice that repayment should begin, and your protests that "I haven't finished yet!" will be disregarded.

College Work-Study (CWS)

The College Work-Study Program provides jobs for students who receive financial aid and who must earn a part of their educational expenses. The federal government pays 70 percent of the salaries, the colleges 30 percent. Students work on an hourly basis in jobs on or off campus and may work during both the academic year and the summer. Although CWS permits students to work up to 40 hours per week, most colleges set lower limits. The amount of your College Work-Study award depends on your financial need and the amount of money your college has for this program. Your pay will be at least the federal minimum wage.

As with SEOG and Perkins loans, you will automatically be considered for this program when you apply for financial aid at a college.

State-by-state program listings

Each state government has established one or more state-administered financial aid programs for qualified students. These state programs may be restricted to legal residents of the state, or they may be available as well to out-of-state students who are attending public or private colleges or universities within the state. In addition, other qualifications may apply.

Filling out the forms

You're fortunate. Just a few years ago, there were half a dozen financial aid forms floating around. It was a nightmare for high school counselors in particular. At my school, we stocked three different kinds and were always short of at least one.

But now, state-, federal- and campus-funded programs are all accessible through the Free Application for Federal Student Aid

(FAFSA). That's right—it's *free*. You can pick one up in the financial aid office of the local community college, or in a high school guidance office. The FAFSA is usually available around Thanksgiving.

You submit a completed FAFSA as soon after January 1 as you can. But not before, or it will be returned you.

You can fill out two-thirds of a FAFSA with no other documents in front of you. Many of the questions asked for information as basic as your home address, age, number of children, and so on.

At some point, however, you will need:

- The US income tax return from the previous year is the most important record. You must use specific numbers from specific lines on the tax return to fill out your application.

You also might need:

- Your parents' return (if you apply as a dependent student).
- Your spouse's return (if you're married and your spouse filed a separate return).

Remember that you may apply even if the tax return is not yet completed. Estimate the financial information on your application. You'll have an opportunity later to change any figures that are incorrect. However, if the process moves along fast, you may have to prove the accuracy of your estimate before you're awarded aid.

Other useful records to have on hand:

- W-2 forms and other records of income received in the previous year.
- Current bank statements and mortgage information.
- Records of benefits received from the Social Security Administration, Department of Veterans' Affairs, and other agencies.

You should save all records and all other materials used to prepare your application because you'll need them later if either the U.S. Department of Education or your school selects you at random for a process called "verification." This means you'll have to prove that what you reported on your application is correct. (Many schools require all financial aid applicants to verify the information they reported.)

As part of the verification process you'll have to give your financial aid administrator certain information or documents, such as the ones mentioned in this section. If you don't provide proof, you won't receive aid from the U.S. Department of Education, and you may not receive aid from other sources. So make sure you keep the documents mentioned, and make sure the information you report is accurate.

Complete your application forms as legibly and neatly as possible, preferably using a typewriter. Use the same legibility and care in preparing all your application documents and letters. Doing so conveys a favorable impression of yourself as a capable, effective person. It also avoids outright errors in deciphering facts about yourself or even functional details like your mailing address.

If you've decided to seek financial aid, make sure that you apply for both admission and financial aid. Applying for admission does not automatically mean you are applying for financial aid. Follow each college's instructions for financial aid applicants precisely. Some colleges have their own "short form" financial aid questionnaire. Fill it out, too, and return it by the deadline—it might be earlier than January 1.

Receiving back a Student Aid Report (SAR)

After you apply for federal student aid, you'll receive a Student Aid Report (SAR) in approximately four weeks. The SAR will contain the information you gave on your application plus numbers that tell you about your eligibility for Federal Student Aid:

- A Pell Grant Index (PG) number, which determines your Pell Grant eligibility.

- Family Contribution (FC) number, used in determining your eligibility for the "campus-based" and Stafford Loan programs.

Unlike the FC, the PGI is a fixed number (below a certain number, you're eligible for a Pell Grant; above a certain number, you're not eligible). This means your SAR can tell you right away about your Pell Grant eligibility. That's why the SAR is most often associated with Pell Grant eligibility, even though it can be used in determining eligibility for other Federal student aid programs.

If your SAR says you qualify for a Pell Grant, your report will have three parts:

- **Part 1—Information Summary.** Contains instructions to review your SAR to make sure it's correct, and will give you other information about the results of your application.

- **Part 2—Information Review Form.** The part you use to change any information on the SAR that's incorrect. Review this part carefully! If you need to make changes, put the correct information in the "The correct answer is" column. Then, sign the certification statement at the end of Part 2. Return Part 2 only to the address given. You'll receive a new SAR in two to three weeks.

- **Part 3—Pell Grant Payment Voucher.** This part is for your school's use.

  If no information on your SAR needs to be changed, submit all three parts of the SAR to your financial aid administrator right away. Your aid administrator will use the information on your SAR to determine the amount of your Pell Grant.

If your SAR says you're not eligible for a Pell Grant, your report will have Parts 1 and 2 only.

But even if your SAR says you're not eligible for a Pell Grant, contact your financial aid administrator. He or she may use the (FC) number on the SAR to determine whether you're eligible for other federal student aid. If you are, your school will send you a letter telling you the amount and kinds of financial aid you'll be offered.

If you have any trouble understanding what you're suppose to do after you get your SAR or how you're supposed to make corrections, your financial aid administrator can help you and can answer any questions you have.

To request a copy of your SAR, write to the agency where you sent your student aid application, or write to the Federal Student Aid Information Center, P.O. Box 84, Washington, D.C. 20044. When you write, make sure you include in your letter your full name, permanent address, Social Security number, date of birth and signature. You can also request a copy of your SAR by calling the telephone number for duplicate requests.

Make sure your correct address is on file, or you won't receive your duplicate SAR. You can correct your address by writing to the agency where you sent your application, or to the Federal Student Aid Information Center. You can't change your address over the phone, however.

Special circumstances

Although the process of determining a student's eligibility for federal student aid is generally the same for all applicants, there is some flexibility.

For instance, if you indicate on your student aid application that you, your spouse, or (if you're a dependent student) either of your parents is a "dislocated worker" or "displaced homemaker," special consideration will be given you and/or their financial status when your application is processed. (For definitions of "dislocated worker" and "displaced homemaker," see your financial aid application.) And, as noted previously, certain applicants with incomes of $15,000 or less can skip some of the questions on the application.

Some students may have special financial considerations that can't be described adequately on an application. If you feel you have special circumstances that might affect the amount you and your family are expected to contribute toward your education, see your financial aid administrator.

Remember, if the aid administrator believes it's appropriate, he or she can change your dependency status from dependent to independent. And, for the campus-based and Stafford Loan programs, the aid administrator may adjust your cost of education or your family contribution if he or she feels your circumstances warrant it.

For example, if you believe the amount you and your family are expected to contribute toward your education is too high, you can ask your aid administrator to review your case. But remember, the aid administrator does not have to make any of these changes—there must be very good reasons for doing so. Also, remember that the aid administrator's decision is final and cannot be appealed to the U.S. Department of Education.

Deadlines

Remember, submit your FAFSA as soon after January 1 as you can. Schools often set deadlines early in the calendar year that students must meet to receive certain types of funds, including campus-based program funds.

The deadline for submitting your SAR to your school's financial aid office is June 30 or your last day of enrollment, whichever comes first. Be sure you know your last day of enrollment; it might be earlier than June 30. The earlier you can submit your SAR, the better, but you must turn it in by the deadline.

Telephone numbers

You may have questions about your student aid application, your SAR or other federal student aid matter, and you need an answer right away. If so, you may call the Federal Student Aid Information Center between the hours of 9 a.m. and 5:30 p.m., Monday through Friday: 800-4-FED AID.

The Information Center provides these services:

- Helps with filing an application or correcting an SAR.

- Checks on whether a school takes part in federal student aid programs, or if a school has a high default rate.

- Explains student eligibility requirements.

- Explains the process of determining financial aid awards.

- Mails publications.

Call 303-722-9200 at the Information Center if you need to find out whether your application has been processed, or if you want another copy of your Student Aid Report (SAR). Please note that you will have to pay for this call. The center cannot accept collect calls.

If you are hearing-impaired, you may call this TDD number, 301-369-0518, at the Information Center for help with any federal student aid questions. This number is not toll-free. The center cannot accept collect calls.

If you suspect any fraud, waste or abuse involving federal student aid funds, call toll-free 800-MIS-USED. It's the hotline to the U.S. Department of Education's Inspector General's office. You may remain anonymous, if you wish.

Guides for financial aid

Chronicle Student Aid Manual. Chronicle Guidance Publications, Inc., Aurora Street, P.O. Box 1190, Moravia, NY 13118-1190.

Revised annually, catalog no. 502A; $19.95 plus $2 postage and handling; or as part of the Educational Subscription at $79.95 plus $8 postage and handling.

The Chronicle Student Aid Annual provides information on financial aid programs available to undergraduate, graduate and postgraduate students. It includes programs sponsored by private organizations and foundations, state and federal government sources, and national and international labor unions. A cross-reference provides easy access to programs for which a student may be eligible. Since the *Annual* is revised, enriched and refined each year, it is most valuable to counselors who seek to keep "up-to-the-minute" in the financial aid field.

Directory of Financial Aid for Minorities, 1994-95. (Gail Ann Schlachter). References Service Press, 1100 Industrial Road, Suite #9, San Carlos, CA 94070. 440 pages, $42.50 hardcover.

This directory provides comprehensive information about the special resources set aside for Asians, Blacks, Hispanics and Native Americans. It lists more than 1,700 financial aid programs, and includes five indexes.

Directory of Financial Aid for Women, 1994-95. (Gail Ann Schlachter), Reference Service Press, 1100 Industrial Road, Suite #9, San Carlos, CA 94070. 425 pages, $42.50 hardcover.

This directory is updated every two years, and is devoted exclusively to listing and cross-referencing scholarships, fellowships, loans, grants, awards and internships that are restricted to women only, women primarily, women and minorities, women and children, institutions serving women, etc. Superbly organized and indexed, it is highly recommended as a reference for women students.

Financial Aid for Veterans, Military Personnel, and Their Dependents, 1994-95. (Gail Ann Schlachter and R. David Weber). Reference Service Press, 1100 Industrial Road, Suite #9, San Carlos, CA 94070. 238 pages, $32.50 hardcover plus $3 for shipping/handling.

Revised every two years, this directory lists more than 600 programs available to qualified personnel, who make up more than one-third of America's population today, for education, research, travel, training career development or emergency situations. It is fully indexed.

Financial Aid for the Disabled and Their Dependents, 1994-95. (Gail Ann Schlachter). References Service Press, 1100 Industrial Road, Suite #9, San Carlos, CA 94070. 230 pages. $32.50 hardcover.

This reference lists more than 800 entries for specialized resources for disabled students, arranged alphabetically and thoroughly indexed.

Don't Miss Out: The Ambitious Student's Guide to Scholarships and Loans. (Robert Leider). Revised annually. Octameron Associates, P.O. Box 3437, Alexandria, VA 22302. $5 plus $1.25 postage and handling.

This booklet is remarkable for the amount of appropriate information about financial aids for college students covered in its pages. It's recommended as an economical, thumbnail resource for students and counselors.

Meeting College Costs, 1995: A Guide for Parents and Students. College Board Publications, Box 886, New York, NY 10101. Free.

This eight-page booklet is revised and updated annually, and offers general guidelines and examples to help students and parents estimate college expenses and compute the expected contributions of parents and students. It also gives information on sources of financial aid, and how to apply for different grants and loans.

Need a Lift? 1995. 44th edition (Terry L. Woodburn, Ed.). Education and Scholarship Commission, National Child Welfare Division, American Legion Headquarters, P.O. Box 1050, Indianapolis, IN 46206. $2 prepaid.

Without doubt, the best reference available for the particular needs of military personnel, the veterans of past wars and conflicts, and their children or orphans, in locating financial aid to education.

Scholarships, Fellowships & Loans (S. Norman Feingold and Marie Feingold). Bellman Publishing Company, P.O. Box 34937, Bethesda, MD 20817. $80.

One of the classic references in this field in its earlier volumes, this guide gives mailing addresses for program sponsors, qualifications (eligibility), funds available, and special fields of interest, and information as added details describing each program.

The Student Guide: Five Federal Financial Aid Programs. Write for a free copy to: Federal Student Aid Programs, Department L-10, Pueblo, CO 81009-0015.

This booklet clearly describes the main federal student financial aid programs—Pell Grants, SEOG, College Work-Study, Perkins Loans, and Stafford and PLUS/SLS Loans—as well as other useful information.

Interviews
Money for those who never say die

Mary Bermingham is proof that many forms of financial aid are available for those who search for them and work to obtain them.

Bermingham began attending college part-time back in 1987. She was also a full-time secretary for an asphalt company, which limited her to night classes.

In 1991 the tables were turned. Bermingham quit her job of 21 years and took on part-time work. This gave her the freedom to increase her college load. She began taking college classes because she wanted to learn to speak French. Once in school, she became interested in the whole school process.

"I loved meeting people and learning," Bermingham said. "I decided to continue taking classes because my son was pretty well grown and I felt confident I could quit my job and still survive.

"I started out with three classes at a time," Bermingham said. "I also signed up with Davis Temporaries to pay for my cost of living. I had real good luck working temporary jobs around my school schedule," Bermingham continued. "I didn't make a lot of money, but it was money."

The truth is, Bermingham didn't really have to make the kind of money it takes to fund a college education. Through constant contact with the financial aid office and a "never-say-die" attitude, she was able to find the funds through scholarships and other financial awards.

Tactics for finding financial aid

Bermingham tried several times to get financial aid through the government. Like many others, she came up empty-handed.

"They look at your past two years of income," Bermingham said. "I had just quit my job, so my income was too high to get even a Guaranteed Student Loan."

However, the asphalt company where Bermingham worked had a profit-sharing program, and she had set up an annuity. She discovered she could draw a certain amount per year from that account without paying a penalty.

"I draw $8,300 per year from that annuity, and will continue to do that until I retire," Bermingham said. "I have to pay income tax on that money, but no penalty charge."

This helped pay Bermingham's college expenses, but she did not quit there. During her three semesters at a community college and four semesters at a university, Bermingham took the opportunity to apply for every scholarship she could find.

When Bermingham transferred out-of-state, she was on an Enrollment Incentive Award Program. This program allows out-of-state students to pay in-state fees for college courses. To qualify for the Enrollment Incentive Award, students must have 60 transferable credits toward their degrees and a grade point average of B or better.

However, Bermingham pointed out that the award does have some restrictions. It only covers 300 and 400 level classes, students can only partake in it four semesters in a row and it doesn't cover summer classes.

"It took planning on my part to make the most of this award," she said. "I made sure to take my prerequisite courses at the community college. Whenever I took something at the community college, I called to make sure it would be accepted at the university. As a result, I haven't taken one class that I haven't been able to use for my degree."

Bermingham also won a number of scholarships during her college years. She said the trick to winning these awards is staying as informed as possible on what is available.

"I made it a point to go into the financial aid office every other week to see what was available," Bermingham said. "It's important for students to keep on top of what's out there and make the best use of every opportunity."

"Most scholarships require a written essay or letters of recommendation," Bermingham continued. "These things take time, but it's worth it."

Financial awards Bermingham received

At the community college:

- **Returning Student Scholarships, $350 each (2).** Bermingham had to fill out an application and write an essay for each.
- **Returning Student Scholarship through the Altrusa Club, $1,000.** The Altrusa Club is the female equivalent of the Masons. Bermingham had to fill out an application, write a short essay and give an acceptance speech at a Club dinner.

At the university:

- **Enrollment Incentive Award.** Bermingham filled out an application and kept her GPA up. She also had to take at least nine credits per semester. She reported she saved approximately $100 per class through this program.
- **Talent Award, $1,000.** This was sponsored by Lever Bros. Co. in Hammond, Indiana. Bermingham filled out an application to get this award. It was spread out over two semesters—$500 each semester.

Bermingham said in spite of all these awards she has won, she was not always successful in obtaining a scholarship or financial assistance. It was her undying effort that allowed her to benefit from financial aid.

"I applied for a lot of scholarships that I didn't get," Bermingham said. "I just kept throwing my line out."

Advice for beginning adult college students

As you can tell, perserverance has a lot to do with landing financial aid. But don't put your energies just into uncovering sources of money: there are other ways of being smart about the costs of education. Here are a few simple strategies Bermingham recommends:

- You have to plan. Every nickel and every hour is important.
- Make sure you don't take classes that don't transfer.
- Keep your GPA up, if not for your own gratification, it makes you more likely to be awarded these scholarships.
- Make yourself aware of what's available at all times through your financial aid office.

Tuition reimbursement helped this returnee

After a brief and unsuccessful attempt at college straight from high school, Shirley Tipsword returned in 1992 to give it another shot. She was 37 at the time.

"I wanted to make myself more marketable," Tipsword said. "With a college degree I would qualify for a higher paying job."

Employee benefits at the osteopathic hospital where Tipsword works do not offer to adjust her schedule to make attending classes possible nor do they offer opportunities in career advancement after completing school. They do, however, include a tuition reimbursement policy.

"They offer partial reimbursement to employees who have been working at the hospital one year," Tipsword said. "After five years they offer up to $1,500 a year for tuition reimbursement."

The plan has fully covered Tipsword's education. The only stipulation for her is that she earn a grade of C or better in all her classes.

"As long as I'm going to school part-time, my tuition doesn't exceed $1,500," Tipsword said. "I work full-time days so I can't attend school full-time anyway.

"I find it frustrating at times that it's taking so long to finish school, but without the reimbursement program I probably would not have returned to school at all," Tipsword said. "I'm really grateful for the policy."

Advice for beginning adult college students

Tipsword said the policy that has paid for her education was in her employee handbook but it wasn't easy to find or understand. She said she had to search it out.

In fact, Tipsword said many other employees that she talked to did not know the policy existed. She advised beginning students to research what their job offers in the way of employee benefits and take advantage of any possible existing policy.

Going back on "a wing and a prayer"

For Ann Marie Cole, the road to higher education was littered with financial tensions.

Cole began her college studies at South Suburban College in Illinois in 1986. She graduated in 1988 with an Associate of Arts degree with an emphasis in English.

"I took out a Guaranteed Student Loan to pay for my college costs," Cole said. "I also worked full-time at a department store and tutored a hearing-impaired student part-time."

After she got her degree, Cole wanted to return to college to get her BA in English, but she couldn't afford the tuition. She already owed money on a Guaranteed Student Loan and didn't qualify for grants and scholarships.

An Enrollment Incentive Award Program allowed Cole to enter Purdue University in 1990. South Suburban College contacted Cole by mail and told her she qualified for the award because of her grade point average.

Cole said the agreement between South Suburban College and Purdue was that all students with a qualifying grade point average did not have to pay out-of-state fees to attend Purdue. However the award program was new, so the guidelines were poorly defined, according to Cole.

"Originally the award included summer school and prerequisites," Cole said. "Then they backed out on the agreement and said the award only covered courses toward the student's majors."

"I attended two other colleges in the same semester because I couldn't afford to pay out-of-state prices for the prerequisites," Cole continued. "I had to work two or three jobs to pay for my education."

Cole did everything from tutoring students to grooming dogs to pay for her schooling. At Purdue, she also worked in the writing center.

While she was still attending Purdue, Cole's Guaranteed Student Loan came due. She paid it off in $55-per-month increments.

"I wanted to leave college debt-free," Cole said. "I was studying to be a teacher, and I knew my salary would not be large enough to handle the burden of student loans."

According to Cole, it's important to be extremely conservative, financially, to afford the expense of college. She took every opportunity to make and save money.

"I always deferred my tuition payments to avoid depleting my bank account," Cole said. "I had to put half down and the other half was not due until one month later."

Cole graduated with honors in the spring of 1993 with a BA in English. Her final grade point average was almost a straight 6.0.

"I went to school on a wing and a prayer," Cole said. "It was very stressful." Her most valuable advice for beginning adult college students? "Be prepared to pay the cost."

It's true—it's unlikely that you're going to locate enough free money to cover all your educational costs. After all, the federal government, which disburses the largest amount of financial aid to students, operates from the premise that it's a family's responsibility to pay for post-high school education. In other words, whenever possible, the burden of paying will be shifted to you: There is no "right" to financial aid, unless you qualify under the guidelines.

You may in fact have to take out a student loan. About 60 percent of students in post-high school programs pay their way with borrowed state and federal money.

But remember, the earnings of a person with a certificate, or a two- or four-year degree, far outstrip that of someone with only a high school diploma. You're making an investment in yourself—and the return is practically guaranteed.

So don't give up because money for school is a little hard to come by. You're as deserving as anyone else in your situation. But you can give yourself a big advantage by making this commitment: "I won't quit—I'm going to keep trying."

Chapter 5

How Will I Juggle Family, Work and School?

You have an advantage as an adult learner:
Time is on your side.

I know what you're thinking: "Time? Time is what I *don't* have. I've already waited this long to go back to school. Now I've got all sorts of responsibilities at home and at work. C'mon! There are just so many hours in a day!"

Right. You understand that only so much can be done in one day, a lesson many younger students—particularly those right out of high school, take awhile to learn.

Ask any dean of college students, for instance, about one of the main reasons undergraduates get poor grades, or even drop out. Odds are he or she will say the reason is poor time management. Young adults in their teens or 20s have a tough time resisting chances to socialize, party or hang out.

But you're beyond that.

You've been hustling to hold a job, meeting commitments you made to yourself or others, and making important choices that are right for you.

If a co-worker were to come up to your desk tomorrow, for instance, and say, "What d'you say we knock off and go out for pizza and beer?", you'd probably respond, "Are you feeling okay? I've got work to do."

But a youngster plowing through a college textbook might respond to the same invitation, "Good idea! I'll just study later tonight."

Something else in your favor—once again having to do with time—is that four-year colleges, community colleges, technical schools, all types of post-secondary educational institutions, are keeping their doors open longer. In addition, many schools offer class schedules that are more creative than the usual quarter or semester formats. As a result, you can better fit your class schedule to your personal and profession commitments.

And speaking of personal commitments, let's take a look at one that's going to be critical to your success, no matter what your educational plans are: the commitment you have to your family.

How you'll need your family's help

First, your partner or family will have to adjust to your not being available as often. Women students seem to feel more role strain over this than men. It's characteristic of women who are trying to combine high prestige careers (or high grade point averages) with family obligations. Added to this, the pressure on a woman to do well at school is great. After all, you fear you're sacrificing the well-being of your family to pursuing your "selfish" goals. Society tends to reinforce this argument, too.

In a study of married re-entry women students, it was found that the longer the woman had been a successful student, the higher her self-esteem; but the longer the woman had been in school, the higher the anxiety experienced by the husband. The more traditional the roles and responsibilities within the family, the greater the guilt the woman experienced about her student role. Other developmental issues for women who return to school include:

- feeling guilty about not "being there" for their children
- concerns about quality and expense of childcare
- minimal individual free time

- feelings of responsibility for maintaining their role within the family

- making compromises in careers because of family considerations

- perceived lack of credibility when returning to college

- insufficient support from family for returning to school

Facing up to the demands of your goals

The role of the successful student requires some degree of selfishness. Call it a "role requirement" of returning to school. Naturally, you'll try to schedule your academic pursuits during the hours that your children are in school, and to confine your studying to solitary time, but there will always be unforeseen emergencies (or unexpected opportunities) that will require you to "rob" family members of your attention—a paper due the next day, or a chance to attend an interesting lecture or seminar in the evening. But if you worry about cooking meals for the family or always "being there" when asked, you'll add to your strain. Ultimately you may seek escape by the route of least resistance—giving up on school.

Instead, learn to value your needs as highly as you value the needs of other people around you. Stand up for your goal. Practice expressing your needs to your family and friends. This is the key to assertive behavior, which is honest, not manipulative, communication.

How to persuade your family to be supportive

When you first look to your family and friends for support in your new venture, you may not find the encouragement you'd hoped for. Many partners see each other as mutual solutions to each other's problems, rather than as individual people with lives, hopes and plans of their own. And it's probably too optimistic to expect a spouse or partner to understand immediately why you need more education for your own sense of fulfillment. After all, he or she may not see the need for it in your situation, especially if children are going to be affected.

So first, work on your own thinking. Emphasize benefits to yourself, not costs. This is a technique psychologists call cognitive restructuring. It could take the form of the following sorts of statements: "I am a better mother for providing my children with a role model of a woman who pursues goals and deals successfully with extra family demands." Or "My children benefit from the fact that my energies are not expended on hovering over them—I allow them chances to practice independence."

Second, plan to compartmentalize your roles. In other words, think in terms of making your being a student as legitimate as your work at home or your career. Think of ways the two roles can be maintained but be distinct. Most of this will depend on time management, which will be discussed later.

Third, push for compromise. If you're a wife or mother, there will be an assumption that you should accommodate your plans to fit around those of other family members. Wives usually expect little from their families in terms of help in adjusting to their career demands, and any sign of accommodation on the part of family members often leaves women feeling guilty. But remember, it's important to teach your children to compromise. You do your best to meet their needs; they need practice at being less dependent on others. It's a part of good parenting, whether you're going back to school, or work or not.

Next, second only in importance to the issue of time spent with family is money. Partners should be open and realistic with each other about the cost of returning to school.

If you're working, you can predict how much more money will be available to the family because of your schooling and what improvements you can look forward to as your career progresses. If you are returning to study full-time, the idea is the same, but it might be a long time before you're back in the work force again earning an income.

If you know what kind of job you are aiming for, try this: Find out the salary level now, add five percent per year over the next five years, and you can estimate what you will be earning then. This is a good technique for persuading the unconvinced that your going back to work or study is a good idea.

In any case, stick to your guns on this point. Anyone in the family who will benefit, financially or in any other way, by the fact that you are going back to school, should be willing to share in the effort of making that possible. No parent or partner is just a domestic support system, a meal-ticket, or the back-up service that enables other people to go off enjoying themselves nonstop. The effort and sacrifice of returning to school should be shared—it's only fair.

But since there are only 24 hours in a day, and family obligations will need to be met, let's return to the issue of time as something you can manage.

Time management is self-management

Your key to coping with most worries and demands connected with juggling work, home and school will be this: You'll have to be very organized day-in and day-out to fit in everything you need to do; but at the same time you will need to be flexible and adaptable enough to reorganize routines and schedules when the unexpected turns up—and it will. You'll have to set boundaries so that your partner and family understand that what you are doing is important and that you are committed to it.

Time management is the art of balancing your efforts, prioritizing what you *could* do as opposed to what you *should* do. It requires you to make choices and postpone short-term gratification for long-term gains. Managing your time means overcoming the bad habits that allow you to put off what needs to be done. It means controlling yourself.

If this sounds intimidating and restrictive, remember this: Time management also eliminates cares and worries. When you do schedule relaxation time—when you deserve to enjoy yourself—you know that you earned it. You're not putting off a chore hoping it will disappear. Things are under control—no need to keep looking over your shoulder. It's a good feeling.

Even now, though, you might be pretty conscientious about being where you're supposed to be and doing what you're supposed to do. You might have a wall calendar near the phone where you pencil in birthdays, performances or appointments. This is time management, all right. But to keep your life balanced while going to school—which is like taking on a part-time job—remember, you can't rely on the family wall calendar. You need a separate one of your own, which will serve as kind of secretary, reminding you of test dates, review sessions, kids' baseball games, no matter where you are.

I suggest you buy a personal planner. You've seen them advertised in magazines; they're sold in office supply stores and department stores, too. But you don't need one that's expensive. Some have leather covers and offer a subscription to refill pages. You could spend as much as $200!

Not necessary. On the other hand, a personal planner is more than a day-by-day spiral for hundreds of daily "to-do" lists. A practical planner—one you'll come to depend on like a good secretary—has these features:

- A month-at-a-glance section. This will allow you to see what's coming up well in advance. Let's say your instructor reminds the class there's a short paper due Monday. You note that in on your monthly calendar, noticing your son has a piano lesson Saturday and you have a committee meeting Sunday after church. All right, budget your time accordingly.

- A day-by-day section. Every day, we all have errands, appointments and so on. The day-by-day section allows you to make "to-do" lists. You can flip ahead a few days and move a task forward to a convenient time slot, if necessary.

  Get into the habit of prioritizing the items on your "to-do" lists. Some people use an A, B, C system, A meaning top priority, C indicating that the item could be moved to another day if necessary. Move forward unfinished tasks to the following day. This creates continuity between one day and the next. Ranking tasks by importance means you'll maximize the use of your time and not waste it on trivialities.

- An address and phone number section. Your classes will bring you into contact with more people—interesting people! Instructors give out their office phone numbers, classmates exchange home and work numbers. You'll discover that having the phone numbers of the library, the bookstore and the registrar's office in your planner is really handy. (Recently, I was registering for classes via an automated phone system. I had to have my PIN—personal identification number—to get into the system. Fortunately, it was in my planner, in the phone number section under P.)

Some planners also have pages for monitoring short-term and long-range goals. In addition, the pockets for business cards, plastic pouches, and pen-holders are useful, too.

All right, now you're armed with your portable time management system—what's next?

Plan all that you can

Sit down with your planner and write in every appointment and activity you already know about. This includes children's lessons, carpool schedules, social events, meetings and deadlines at work—everything.

I'm a single parent with two children, ages 12 and 10, and there are weekly obligations I know about at home and work, so I have them written in my monthly calendar: I don't try to carry them in my head from week to week. Here are some items that are "in stone" on my calendar—ones I have to schedule classes around:

- Department meetings are every Monday and Thursday at 3 p.m.
- Andrew has a piano lesson at 7 a.m. Wednesdays.
- I have to pick up neighborhood kids from choir at 4:30 Wednesdays.
- Andrew has gymnastics Wednesdays at 6 p.m.
- Andrew has choir at 7:30 a.m. on Fridays.
- Lauren has an oboe lesson at 1 p.m. Saturday.

In addition, Lauren has volleyball games sprinkled hither and yon throughout the month, so those go in my planner, too.

Looking over these commitments, I scheduled classes for these times this quarter:

> Mondays: 4:30 - 6 p.m.
> Tuesdays: 6:00 - 8:30 p.m.
> Saturdays: 9:00 a.m. - noon

On my calendar, I've also written in "Grandma" every Tuesday, reminding me that my mother comes on Tuesday to watch the kids and make dinner while I'm in class (I like to have the house looking reasonably clean before she arrives).

Now, if everything I've said so far seems pretty obvious, I'm only trying to reiterate an important point: The first objection or concern someone else might raise about your going back to school will be something like, "Where will you find the time?" Meaning, "How will you meet other people's expectations and still go to school?"

As I pointed out earlier, for your part, you should expect support from your family. Families should be places where people can grow—but I caution you not to demand that loved ones sacrifice too much. You're a parent, a spouse, a partner, a colleague: These are relationships where trust is involved.

Let me give you a personal example of how I made trouble for myself and others by believing I could do everything.

A few years ago, I persuaded myself that I really could do it all. It was just a matter of better time management (which really meant sleeping less, actually). The crisis came when a friend asked me to audition for a lead role in a community theater play. Now, I like to perform—I don't get stage fright—so I said I'd be glad to. Never mind the long, long rehearsals; the tediousness of doing the same thing over and over; the strain on my kids of having to do their homework in an empty theater. No, this was going to provide "relaxation."

I got the part, but close to opening night, after two months of rehearsals, a strange thing began happening. I started drawing a complete blank when it was my turn to speak. I had trouble remembering the way the third act was supposed to go. My cues, my entrances—all of it—faded into a mysterious fog. I stood in the wings getting panicky. About the fourth time I muffed a big scene because I hadn't the slightest idea what my lines were, the director took me aside. "Why can't you remember—what's happening?" she asked. I told her I had this funny feeling I didn't know where I was: I felt anxious about having to be someplace else—but I wasn't sure where.

Talk about role confusion! I was having trouble separating my "role" as a person playing a character, from my other roles as dad, teacher, responsible grown-up: I couldn't concentrate long enough to get through six minutes of pretend dialog.

So keep your obligations in mind. Planning your time so that others can depend on you is an act of consideration.

Here are 10 tips to keep you on track as your juggle responsibilities.

1. Keep the vision of your goal in front of you. If your hopes and wishes come to pass, how do you see yourself? Walking across the stage at commencement and receiving your diploma? Or taking a new job with a new office? Or making more money? If a photograph symbolizes your dream—an open, tropical beach or a shot of a fashion design studio—post it where you'll see it frequently.

2. Turn your vision into written goals and objectives. "By 1997 I will have finished my work for my degree. I'll take two courses each fall and winter term over the next four years, and in the last year, I will go full-time to finish my remaining course work. I will receive my diploma June 1997."

This is a good goal statement because it has been translated into measurable objectives.

3. Always plan on paper. If it's not written on paper (or in a computer), it's not a plan; it's only an idea. If it's not written out, it just doesn't get properly developed and executed. Your plan can be brief: maybe a step-by-step outline of what you want to do, by when, and how—that's all. But the important thing is keeping your plan before your eyes. This is a map of your future you're drawing for yourself. Think about it: Which would you prefer?

Verbal directions on how to reach some distant point—"Turn left, turn right, go 12 miles"—or a map? Be a smart navigator through unknown waters: keep the plan prominently in front of you. Put it on your mirror; stick it up on the fridge; or carry it in your planner all during your journey.

4. Create an organization center. Working at the kitchen table and putting your paper and handouts each night won't do. Turn a closet, a spare room, a corner of the kitchen into your office space, equipped with the tools of school: pencils, pens, paper clips. In short, give yourself a business-like space to work in.

5. Approach projects with a step-by-step action plan. Call it "Organizing for Success." This is more than a "to-do" list. It's linking actions to goals. Let's say, for example, you have a major paper due. More than writing "Big Paper Due" under a date on your calendar, write out action steps like these:

- Review assignment in syllabus and talk with professor to determine dimensions of assignment and learn criteria for grade of A.
- Choose a topic.
- Read background material.
- Develop an outline.
- Conduct research.
- Assemble notes and integrate them into outline.
- Write and edit first draft.
- Write and edit second draft.
- Produce final copy.
- Submit paper to professor.

Action step-by-step planning defines all the tasks to be done and the time frame in which they are to be completed.

6. Share your vision with others. If no one knows what you're attempting to do, they have no way to help you achieve your goals. Even if people can't actively help you achieve your goals, they can keep you from being successful without intending to.

Involving others in your efforts will motivate them to want you to succeed, especially if they know how to help. Of course, some people may be jealous or resentful of your efforts. Perhaps your spouse or your children resent your inability to spend as much time with them now and dislike having to do for themselves things that you used to do for them. Perhaps a fellow employee will see you getting ahead while he or she is not. Even your boss may fear that your success will eventually come at his or her expense.

For the most part, though, people will want to help you succeed. If they know your visions, your goals and your plans, they will join you on your journey. If you do not ask for their help, especially if your plans affect them, they may well feel resentment.

7. Develop flexible standards. There is a significant difference between having flexible standards and lowering your standards. Many tasks creep into your daily routine because you have the time to do them or because you enjoy doing them.

Once you're in school, you may clean your house less often or less thoroughly. You may wash the car less frequently. You may set aside a hobby or project. At work, you may volunteer for fewer committee assignments, write fewer memos about things that don't interest you, and may not be available to all drop-in visitors. You may eat lunch at your desk so you can finish work that you used to take home in a briefcase at day's end but that now competes with the homework you have to do at night.

All things must pass, and this period of double-duty—school and work, school and home—will pass, too. In the meantime, try not to heap criticism on yourself for not doing things perfectly. Perfectionism is not a direction you personally want to go in, in any case.

8. Learn to delegate. Children will learn to make their own lunches. Co-workers will pick up special projects if you ask. A fast-food chain will be glad to do your cooking, and if you can afford it, others will be glad to clean your home, change the oil in your car and mow your lawn. Think about what you don't need to do.

9. Say no! Here's a test: If asked to do something, consider whether agreeing to will help you personally or professionally. If not, say no. If that's too harsh for you, offer to swap your time for someone else's, as in "I'll watch your children this afternoon if you'll watch mine tomorrow."

10. Reward yourself. Keeping your nose to the grindstone creates neither a sharp grindstone nor an appealing-looking nose. Work when you're supposed to work; play when you deserve or need it.

Interview
Learn to maximize your time

For Tammy Vergara, postponing her college degree was an accident. In fact at the age of 8, she'd already made a vow to go to college someday.

"I always knew I would go to college," Vergara said. "Seeing my mom go through a divorce made me realize how important it is to be self-sufficient."

However, family difficulties made it impossible for Vergara to attend college straight from high school. At 23, she finally began working toward her degree.

"I was typically older than everyone in my classes," Vergara said. "There were times when I felt frustrated because I didn't have much in common with other students."

Vergara did not let this age difference discourage her, though. She graduated with honors in 1993 from Purdue University with a BA in communications.

"I knew that it was up to me to do the work and I would be rewarded," Vergara said. "The opportunities open mainly for those who are willing to try."

Vergara said her previous real-life experience gave her an advantage over those who entered college immediately from high school. "I don't think 17- and 18-year-olds are capable of assessing what they want to do—especially in this age of technology and information, where things are constantly changing," she said.

Juggling work and school

Vergara was not yet married when she began college in 1988. She worked full-time at a label company and went to college part-time.

The label company was a small operation of approximately 50 to 75 employees. There were no back-to-school incentives or even encouragement from management. As administrative assistant and personnel manager, Vergara was the person who could have proposed and written a policy that would give employees the incentive and ability to return to school and work at the same time. At the time, however, the company had no need for a policy of that kind, predominantly due to its small size.

In spite of this, when Vergara returned to college part-time, company officials made amends by allowing her to leave early on certain nights to get to classes on time. She was able to complete two years of college as a part-time student in this manner.

Juggling marriage and school

When Vergara married in 1991, her husband, Frank, knew that college was a priority for her.

"Frank was extremely understanding because he had gone through eight years of college to earn his doctorate in optometry," Vergara said. "He knew I was going to have to put a lot of myself into my studies."

Vergara said the time constraints brought on by the demands of a college workload were hard to accept, but she and her husband made the most of their time together.

"We learned to maximize our time," Vergara said. "Instead of going our own direction, we'd spend quality time with each other."

In fact, Vergara and her husband developed a ritual to ease the frustration brought on by these constraints. Every Friday night they created a romantic setting, let the answering machine answer the phone and relaxed.

"One of us would rent a movie and pick up a bottle of wine during the day," Vergara said. "Then at night we'd make a fort out of comforters and pillows, light a fire, drink our wine and watch the movie."

Vergara said not only was her husband extremely understanding and supportive during her college years, he also made great financial sacrifices. In fact, she said he put a lot of his own plans on a back burner so she could pay for college.

Vergara said now she and her husband will start saving so he can reach his goal of opening an optometry practice. Although she'd like to attend graduate school as soon as possible, she said that will only happen if her employer pays the expense.

"Frank postponed his plans long enough," Vergara said. "I don't feel I should ask him to wait any longer."

Time management

Vergara linked her success in college to effective time management. She said planning out her time left little room for chance.

"I always mapped my time out by the week and by the day," Vergara said. "Sometimes I mapped out my month or my entire semester, depending on how hectic things were."

"I always knew at any given time what I needed to accomplish in a day, in a week, in a month and, at times, in the whole semester," Vergara said. "I don't think I could have survived if I hadn't."

Studying habits

For Vergara, the secret to studying was to be thorough and to take frequent breaks. "The magic number for me was six to eight hours of study per test," she said. "I wouldn't allow myself to study something for more than an hour without taking a break," Vergara said. "I'd do this until I had studied six to eight hours."

Vergara said she never stopped studying until she felt saturated. "I continued until I couldn't take in any more information," she said.

Vergara also had a unique method for writing papers. She went through a methodical procedure to organize her thoughts and brainstorm, then she checked her writing style and grammar with a list of items that she created.

"First I wrote ideas down," Vergara said. "Then I organized the ideas, plotting them in a circular form around the middle, central idea. After I brainstormed for a while, I free wrote. Then I checked for grammatical and stylistic errors."

"By doing this, eventually I didn't need as much revision," Vergara said. "I developed the habit of checking these things as I was writing."

Reading textbooks presented another challenge for Vergara. Like many adult college students, she found textbook reading extremely different from the casual reading she was used to.

"To read textbooks, I first looked at the chapter to see how long it was," Vergara said. "Then I read the subtitles. Then I would read leisurely," Vergara continued. "All the while I was reading, I highlighted the important points."

To study the reading, Vergara paraphrased each highlighted point on a separate sheet of paper. She then took these notes and highlighted the important points in her notes.

"I did this until I condensed my notes down to two to three pages," Vergara said. "It got to the point where I would remember not only what page of the book the information was on, but exactly where it was on the page."

Advice to beginning adult college students

- "Don't take on more than you know you can handle. If you're working full-time, don't start out with three or four classes. Take one class, and if you feel comfortable, take two or three the next semester. If you don't take on more than you can handle, you'll enjoy your college education—and you should enjoy it."

- "Don't focus on the whole thing. Take it in segments. Take it a year at a time. If you can focus on manageable chunks, before you know it your college education will be over. Don't allow yourself to be overwhelmed."

Chapter 6

Will I Have Trouble Making the Grade?

A frequent nightmare among adults is finding themselves back in school and being unprepared for a final exam, or failing a class. Thus it's not surprising that one of the biggest fears many adults confront when considering returning to school is that they won't be able to make the grade. That their rusty study skills will not be adequate. That they no longer know how to do homework, answer multiple-choice questions, read textbooks, write papers, or study for tests. That they will wake up one morning only to remember they have a term paper due and a final exam scheduled—for a class they've neglected to attend all semester.

The reality is a little different—and a lot more optimistic. The truth is, as an adult, you probably utilize the same skills required for study in your job or home life on an everyday basis. Skimming reports for key information in preparing for an important meeting, crafting a memo that will convince your boss that you're the person to take on a new account, reading and following instructions for enrolling your child in camp or operating the VCR—even something as routine as remembering the items you were supposed to pick up at the grocery—are the types of activities that have kept your study skills polished to a high gloss.

So don't panic. You're already smarter than you think. But, just to reassure you, consider this chapter a refresher course for the study skills you'll need to make your back-in-school experience a success.

How to get the most out of your classes

Going to school involves more than coming to class and handing in assignments: Listening, participating, and taking notes are vital.

- Listen actively, not passively. Think about what the teacher is saying; anticipate where he or she is going. Listen for reinforced information through clues like, "As I've pointed out..." "Now this next idea is especially interesting..." As you know, it's possible to hear without really thinking. Compare the teacher's ideas with those you already have. After all, you're not going to school to "relearn" what you already know.

- Take notes sparingly. Don't write down everything. Notes are memory-joggers about important ideas. Develop your own personal shorthand. Let your system develop gradually so you don't confuse yourself. Here are some examples:

t = the	< = less than
w/ = with	> = more than
+ = and	+ = increase
- = decrease	gov = government
s = supply	U = union

Getting along well with instructors

College instructors enjoy seeing adults in class—you bring experience and maturity. So try to put aside your old attitudes of awe or resentment toward teachers, which might still be hanging on from your previous school years. This is a clean slate you're starting with.

Another difference worth thinking about is this: Teachers in higher education like to discuss ideas—ideas that challenge their own, too. You're not expected to sit quietly and agree with everything you hear. Participate! Take on a popular opinion; explain how your life experiences have influenced your beliefs. The only rule is that you respect the views of others and demonstrate tolerance.

You might also decide to continue your studies and you'll need recommendations from your instructors for graduate programs, honors seminars, and other opportunities. Speak up in class and go the extra mile with your assignments. These are ways you can guarantee strong recommendations from your instructors.

And last, be careful not to fall behind in your assignments. Ask your instructor for help as soon as you find yourself in any difficulty. This will enable you to catch up before you've fallen behind. But problems aren't the only reasons to talk with your professor. If you're doing well in a course, you may want to discuss topics that especially interest you. Sharing interests and enthusiasm in your studies with your professors is one of the main satisfactions and benefits of college study.

Starting a study group

Making new friends is also something to look forward to when returning to school. An easy way to make several friends at once is by starting a study group.

It's really a kind of support group—members have a common goal: everyone's success. By comparing and contrasting course notes, covering for one another when one of you can't attend class, and generally watching out for one another's interests, the group is a practical and personal resource. In fact, studies have shown that students who have at least one other person on campus who is sincerely interested in their success have a greater potential for success than loners do.

A study group will also provide you with multiple points of view about what's important; help you clarify what you don't understand; focus on likely test questions; even act as editors and share responsibility for assisting one another in the development of papers, projects or difficult assignments. And the best thing is, "study buddies" provide encouragement.

Don't be shy about forming a group: Others will appreciate your taking the lead. Just pass around a sheet of paper headed "Want to be in a study group? Put your name and phone number below." Be careful, though—you might end up with half the class on your list. Circulate the sign-up sheet among half-a-dozen class members as a trial.

Hold your first meeting in a neutral, easy to find location like the college library or cafeteria. Later, you might volunteer your home on an evening or a Sunday afternoon. Before you know it, your study group will be a big part of your back-in-school lifestyle.

Hitting the books on your own: Study tips

You, like most of your fellow students who are returning to school, are probably a working person. Buckling down to several hours of homework—sometimes just thinking about doing the homework—will be hard.

Well, ask yourself these tough questions: Am I willing to put effort into my goal to get a degree? Am I willing to make some sacrifices now in order to achieve my goal? There's no shortcut to learning. When you find yourself making excuses—"This teacher expects too much of a working person." "Adults shouldn't have to do homework." "I'm just too busy to study"—remember, you need to put in time at home or at the library to do justice to your classes. Otherwise, you're going to a lot of trouble for a meager result: a grade.

Since your time is limited, however, here are some tips for maximizing the effort you spend on homework:

Study in the right place: a room in your home, a study carrel at the local library—anyplace there are no distractions. Don't get too comfortable, though. A deep easy chair may make you drowsy. Try a straight-backed chair with a table. Also, find good lighting. Adopt a business-like attitude toward your work.

Study at the right time. Studying an hour in the morning when you're rested is worth two in the evening when you're beat. Schedule unbroken periods when you can be productive; build-in some natural breaks, about every half hour or hour, to stretch and relax.

Study with a method in mind. Follow these steps when you are getting ready to read a book or other material for class:

- Take a few minutes to preview a book or reading assignment. Look through the publication information, the table of contents and the index.
- Now page through the reading assignment. Read the main headings and subheadings. What is the topic covered by each subsection?

- Now that you know the main points the author wants to cover, read the material. Read for the important ideas. When you come to an especially important idea, pause and repeat it to yourself. Play "Jeopardy" by posing a question with a date, name or concept as the answer.

- Take notes as you read. As you come to important points, write them down. Remember that each paragraph usually has only one important idea, and this may or may not be important for you. There is no need to write down long, involved sentences, however. Keep your sentences simple and short. This will help you to remember.

- When you come to a word or concept that you don't know, and you think it may be important for the meaning of your reading, jot it down on a piece of paper. Look up the work in a dictionary; look up the concept in a glossary in the back of the book, or take it to class and ask about it. But don't just skip words or terms you don't understand.

- One of the most important parts of study comes after you have read the assignment. Take your notes and read them over. This helps fix the ideas in your mind. Review them again before you begin another study period. Spacing out your studying puts information into long-term, as opposed to short-term, memory.

Taking an exam

Knowing how to take an exam is as important as knowing how to study.

There are different kinds of written exams. There are essay exams, which require you to write an appropriate full answer to the question and demonstrate your understanding of the question and the material, as well as short-answer exams, which require some writing, from a few words to several sentences. In addition, there are multiple-choice exams, which require careful reading and the selection of one of several choices of answers. Your teacher may give you one kind or a combination of these kinds of exams.

First, ask your instructor ahead of time what the exam will cover. This is fair game. He or she might tell you to concentrate on certain topics, or preview the format of the test: so many essay questions, so many fill-in-the-blanks.

On the day of the test, read the whole exam through first. Start on sections that will take the most time. Leave the easy questions, like true/false, to the end when you're pressed to get finished.

Next, read each question carefully. Your first step is to be sure you understand the question. For instance, one question might ask you to *list* several possible causes of infection, and another might ask you to *describe* several possible causes of infection. Notice the critical difference in the words "list" and "describe." Other common critical words you will find in exams are: explain, evaluate, compare, elaborate on, defend, and identify.

A good practice to adopt before writing a short or long answer is to list in the margin ideas you want to cover. This serves as a quick outline.

On multiple-choice questions, trust your judgment. Your first hunch is probably the best, but read all the choices. Don't jump at the decoy answers that sound approximately right at first glance.

Check your test over before handing it in. This is not a contest. There are no awards for finishing first.

Writing a short paper

Writing a short paper is a routine assignment in college. It will require some limited research, and it will challenge your ability to organize facts and make yourself clear. Here's a step-by-step approach:

Step 1: Choose a topic that interests you. Clear the it with the instructor. Check to make sure you will have access to research resources you may need.

Step 2: Write the rough draft. At this point, don't worry about sentence order, wording, grammar or spelling—just get down ideas to work with.

Think of your paper as consisting of three parts:

An introduction. This clarifies the topic in your own and the reader's mind. Among the many kinds of introductions you can use are:

- A statement of purpose (example: "The purpose of this paper is...")

- A statement of intent (example: "The intent of this paper is to prove...")

- A brief history of your topic (example: "The origins of slavery can be traced to...")

- A definition of you topic (example: "An 'escalator clause' is...")

A body. This is the longest part of the paper and develops your ideas or makes your case. List on a piece of paper the most important ideas or points you want to present. There might be only a couple, or a dozen or more. If your paper is long and detailed, you might also list subpoints. Review your points to make sure they're presented in a logical, understandable order. Each main topic or point deserves at least a paragraph of explanation.

A conclusion. It should be short. Here are several ways of concluding a paper. Summarize your main points; make a general assessment of the situation described in your paper; offer your opinion about the topic; propose a solution to a problem presented in the body of your paper, or at least highlight aspects that deserve more attention.

Step 3: Now rewrite the three parts of your paper, *but it's a good idea to put a paper aside between drafts*. You'll come back to it with fresh insights. Moreover, portions that are unclear will be obvious to you. A good "road test" of your work is to read it aloud to someone else. If it sounds confusing or wordy, it probably is. Good writing, as the British novelist Virginia Woolf said, reads like good conversation. Strive to sound as much like an average speaker as you can.

Writing a research paper

A research paper depends much less on opinion than an essay or a short paper does. Instead, it summarizes what has already been said or written on a particular subject. The aim is to present a comprehensive picture of what is known about a topic. This requires getting information from various sources and putting this information together in a logical, coherent, original way. Sources may be books, periodicals, newspaper articles, original documents, and interviews. Often, research papers require the additional skills of creating, comparing, analyzing, and judging ideas.

Because you'll be gathering a lot of information for a research paper, here are some tips for organizing it:

- Keep a complete record on index cards of the books and magazines you look at. You will need this information later for footnotes and bibliography. For books include author, title, place of publication, publisher, date and inclusive page numbers. For magazines include article author, article title, magazine title, volume number, date and inclusive page numbers.

- Take notes: Put your notes on cards, only one idea per card. Use your own words and be as brief as possible. If you plan to quote an author, put his or her exact words on the card with quotation marks around them. Always indicate the source and page on each note card, so you can footnote it if you use it in your paper.

- Rewrite the description of your topic, if necessary. You may find that your ideas about your subject have changed. This will guide you as you organize your paper.

- Make an outline for your paper from your notes. Sort your note cards into groups, each group a main section of your paper. Organize each group into the main points of your paper. This is a logical method of creating an general outline that will guide your writing.

- Reference quotes and ideas by footnotes. A direct quote is an exact, word-for-word copy of another writer's words.

Use a direct quote mainly when an idea is expressed so concisely and well that you can't improve on it, or a remark is peculiar. Put quotation marks around the material if it is short; if it's more than four or five lines, indent it as a block. Always footnote a direct quote.

An indirect quote is material from another source that has been paraphrased or reworded. When you want to express an idea similar to the way someone else has expressed it, but not word-for-word, use an indirect quote. Don't use quotation marks, but footnote the reference. The tricky aspect of indirect quotes is that you run the risk of plagiarism, which is using someone else's ideas without giving credit. When in doubt, footnote.

Making the grade

A big part of succeeding in school is being organized. Regardless of your abilities, by planning your work, checking your understanding, and being prepared for class and for tests, you'll go a long way toward realizing the kind of academic success you had hoped for by going back to school.

Interview
Learn some organizational skills

After struggling in the field of music for 17 years, Ann Curtis entered a Midwestern university in 1987 to prepare for a more lucrative career. She was 27 years old.

"I entered college blind," Curtis said. "I had no idea what to expect."

Curtis didn't expect to have difficulty with such simple things as taking notes and reading textbooks. Even so, she found herself spending hours trying to read one simple chapter and make sense of her notes.

"I was getting straight As, but it was killing me," Curtis said. "For a while I suspected that I had some kind of analytical disability."

What Curtis discovered, through talking to other students, was that her problem was not uncommon. Many other students in her classes complained of similar difficulties.

"I realized there was a method to reading text books," Curtis said. "I was approaching them as I had the classics I loved so well before entering college."

Curtis went to the library for help with her problem. She checked out several books on study habits.

"The books were really just full of practical information," Curtis said. "The techniques they suggested made sense to me."

"Most of the books advised students to peruse each chapter before actually reading it," Curtis continued. "This involved noting the length of the chapter, reading the subtitles and reviewing any summary questions that might be listed at the end of the chapter."

Although the books helped, Curtis went one step further. She discovered that the college sometimes offered a night class on how to study, so she attended the class.

"I was surprised at how many simple tactics could alleviate the burden of studying," Curtis said. "The class was a definite benefit."

Curtis said she learned organizational skills in the class. The teacher recommended that students use different colored pencils when taking notes to keep different ideas separate.

In addition, Curtis, a Spanish major, learned to use index cards as she read to keep track of vocabulary words. She also discovered how to use a highlighter effectively.

"I was one of those who would highlight every sentence in the chapter," Curtis said. "By learning how to summarize the chapter and recognize the important points, I was able to break that habit."

"After attending the class, I was also able to make my notes much more organized," Curtis continued. "It made a recognizable difference."

Curtis graduated in 1993 with a BA in Spanish international studies and public relations. Her final grade point average was 5.9 out of 6.0.

Advice for beginning adult college students

- "Take the time to learn some organizational skills that will work for you. It will help you decipher your notes when you need them. Also, review your notes immediately after class. Fill in the gaps from memory, or ask another student for help."

- "Don't try to read a college text book leisurely, as you would a novel. It just doesn't work. Skim the material first. Break it down into topics."

- "It's also very important to read the summary questions at the end of each chapter. These will lead you toward the information you need. Keep these questions in mind while reading the chapter."

- "While you're reading the chapter, take sparse notes. Whether in class or at home reading, do not take so many notes that you are overwhelmed."

- "Give yourself plenty of time to review notes when preparing for a test."

- "Talk to other students. Find out what note-taking and reading techniques work for them."

- "Take advantage of courses on studying techniques if you have access to them at your university. They could make your entire school experience more enjoyable."

Chapter 7

How Will I Make More Education Work for Me?

For many returning students, the purpose of going back to school is career advancement. The goal is not only receiving a degree or certificate, but also acquiring the skills and education for work that's more satisfying. Completing your program of study is a step forward on your career path.

A career, incidentally, is not the same as a position or job. A career is a sequence of positions occupied by a person during the course of a lifetime.

Your additional education may lead to a significant *career change*. Career change is an occupational shift—not merely from one job to another—but a change in the actual work a person does. Examples of a career change are a painter becoming a drafter; a pharmacist becoming a lawyer; a lawyer becoming a teacher.

The process of making a change may be as basic as using new skills and credentials for advancement within the same company and career field. Or as complex as making a radical career change.

In any case, deciding on the next step in your career takes time. You might be on your third or fourth major job, none of them really related. Until you find a career direction that calls to you,

you may feel dissatisfied, uncertain and lost. These are common feelings—many people have them.

Likewise, if you don't know exactly why you want to go off in a new direction, that's okay, too. At midlife, there is no single factor that motivates someone to make a career move, although researchers have identified several reasons for it:

- Financial circumstances. Having more money increases the opportunities for making a career change at midlife.

- Self-concept. Having a high self-concept increases the likelihood of career change.

- Personal meaning. A desire to find more personally meaningful work often leads to career change. A study showed that 76 percent of men between the ages of 34 and 54 who had changed high-status careers said they wanted to find more meaningful work, and 69 percent said they wanted a better fit between their values and their work.

- Interests. Incompatible interests with a current career often lead to dissatisfaction in the workplace.

- Beliefs. Persons who have a strong desire to control their lives are more likely to make a career change at midlife.

Do any of these reasons sound similar to yours?

Who you are and the work you want to do

Let's assume that you do want to discover work that satisfies you—work that brings excitement, prestige and a sense of fulfillment. Good! To begin your vocational discovery process you need to look at your personal values and interests. You need to clarify what you want from life and look at the job market—to find a match between what you enjoy doing and what the world needs.

This is the fun part of the process: itemizing important things about yourself. Make two columns on a piece of paper. One column should be headed "Values" and the other "Skills."

First, what do you value in life? The older you get, the more your career decisions will be based on your values (I have a theory that mature persons have the courage to say what they want without worrying other people won't approve).

Some of the work-related values people often have are these:

- Helping people or improving the world.

- Being the boss, having power and influence over others.

- Enjoying security, understandable work and steady paycheck.

- Responding to excitement, challenge and pressure.

- Making money enough to live "the good life."

- Being allowed to choose one's own work and standards.

- Being creative: bringing beauty, variety and new ideas into the world.

In addition, personal satisfactions from your work—other than money—might include:

- Working with things or information instead of people.

- Being in a pleasant environment, wearing good clothes.

- Working outdoors.

- Working as part of a friendly team.

- Performing a service of value to others.

Now take a moment to reflect on jobs you have had in the past. What were the qualities you really liked or valued? What were the things you could do without? Remember, no job is perfect. List the drawbacks you've encountered at the bottom of your "Values" column.

All right, let's move over to the "Skills" column.

Every person has many skills. Adding to your education gives you even more. You might be good at communication, juggling figures, fixing things with your hands or being sensitive to people's needs. So identify your skills. Let your friends help—you might be too modest or unaware of some things you do well.

Some skills that employers prize are:

Budget management	Supervising
Handling deadline pressure	Interviewing
Negotiating/arbitrating	Communicating
Getting along with people	Public relations
Information gathering	Instructing

What to do if you're stuck

When I was thinking about a major career change some years ago, I decided to make sure I was going about the process the right way. Just weighing my options wasn't enough—I wanted to become a little bit of an expert on myself as a worker and how to reach my goals.

If you're like this, too, I recommend you pick up one or several of the following books and just learn the "language" of career exploration. You'll feel more confident about what you're doing as a result. Here are some first-rate career planning books:

What Color is Your Parachute? by Richard Nelson Bolles (Ten Speed Press). This is still probably the best and most comprehensive career-assessment book available, with numerous self-help exercises, and excellent information on interviewing, hiring practices and understanding the total job search.

Shifting Gears by Carole Hyatt (Fireside Books). A guide to the early steps of looking inward and discovering what you really want to be doing.

Wishcraft by Barbara Sher and Anne Gottlieb (Ballantine Books). Another well-known book on career changing—this one focuses on building a team of supporters or a professional network to help you.

The Age of Unreason by Charles Handy (Harvard Business School Press). A fascinating look at the future of the American workplace and the American worker. Chapter 3 offers revealing self-assessment exercises.

Kiplinger's Take Charge of Your Career by Daniel Moreau (Kiplinger Books). Practical advice about everything from coping with being fired to interviewing well.

Counseling Midlife Career Changes by L.J. Bradley (Garrett Park Press). This readable book for career changers and counselors offers a practical approach to problems and situations involving midlife career changes through numerous case examples of exercises. Career counselors have many ways to help you discover an exciting new career path.

Do the exercises in these books; highlight passages that seem important to you. Any important choice in life deserves this kind of attention.

Here are some first-rate books about careers in general (see Appendix 3, too):

Job Hunter's Resources Guide. Gale Research, Inc. The central part of this guide is "Sources of Job Hunting Information: 150 Professions and Occupations," which lists job-hunting manuals, directories, employment agencies, placement services, trade journals with help-wanted ads and other information services.

Jobs '93 by Kathryn & Ross Petras. Prentice Hall Press. Excellent career opportunity source book for the '90s. Gives career outlooks, industry forecasts and regional round-ups to keep the reader appraised of the most current trends and where they are creating jobs.

Occupational Outlook Handbook. The U.S. Department of Labor, Bureau of Labor Statistics. This is an excellent source book for vocational guidance. It describes the nature of what workers do in each job listed, the training and education they need, earnings, working conditions and expected job prospects for selected occupations covering a wide cross-section of the economy.

Peterson's Job Opportunities for Business and Liberal Arts Graduates. Peterson's Guides. Helps recent college graduates with their job hunting by providing an overview of the various types of employment opportunities available with 400 corporations that are planning to hire business and social sciences/humanities graduates.

Getting a second opinion: Career services

On the other hand, you might get through reading a popular book on career planning, and still not understand yourself any better. In other words, you understand the process, but you don't know where *you* fit in.

Then it's time to get a second opinion—maybe some expert advice, too.

Your college, university or trade school probably has a career counseling and placement office. This is more than a collection of books—it's an excellent resource for you.

First, if the counseling center is staffed by a professional career counselor, he or she can help you clarify your values; understand your own decision-making process; identify your skills; analyze your past and present career experiences; and find and use career information. In addition, he or she may offer you career preference tests, career aptitude tests, or suggest that you join a career planning group or workshop.

Career aptitude and interest batteries can be especially useful. Just by expressing your work preferences or by answering a series of questions, you will receive a profile about yourself. You might indicate, for instance, that most of your work interests and values fall within the business world—or you might reveal an aptitude in mechanical understanding you didn't realize you had.

Here are some popularly used career interest and aptitude tests, and some software programs for career exploration:

Strong-Campbell Interest Inventory (SCII)
An occupational interest inventory comparing students' answering patterns with those of people satisfactorily employed in various occupations. Questions deal with likes/dislikes; norms based on a population of four-year degree, professional employees. Probably more suited to students with interest in professional fields requiring at least a four-year degree.

Career Assessment Inventory (CAI)
Similar in format to the Strong-Campbell, this assessment is normed on the general population. It is usually more suitable for students in vocational education.

Self-Directed Search (SDS)
This is a self-evaluating, less formal inventory. Categories cover areas of interest and competencies.

Discover
A complete, computerized career planning system features a nine-step sequence covering all aspects of career planning, with an emphasis on a graphic/visual approach.

Minnesota Importance Questionnaire (MIQ)
Vocational inventory in which test-takers are asked to rank job statements; thus indicating features important to their ideal job. Assists in prioritizing values and predicting job satisfaction.

California Occupational Preference System (COPS)
A self-administered and self-scored inventory, comparing relative strength of interest in many different occupations. Provides print-out of college majors. Available for different reading levels.

Myers-Briggs Type Indicator, Edwards Personal Preference Schedule, Personality Research Form (PRF)
These are personality profiles, indicating personality types. They help to understand how students perceive information and life.

Personality Mosiac
This checklist inventory rates your likes and dislikes in these categories: data, people and things (objects, machines).

Please Understand Me
(Jefferson Software)
Results are similar to Myers-Briggs Personality Profile. Can be completed on a computer, or with pencil and paper. Used primarily as self-awareness tool.

System of Interactive Guidance and Instructions (SIGI)
Computerized occupational assessment and exploration system in nine steps. Usually, the first section can be completed in approximately two hours. This system has in-depth research potential including values clarification and resume help.

As a result of your career exploration, you might hit on a list of occupations that fit well with your values, aptitudes, goals and education.

But watch out—don't be misled by glamour, or other distractors. Many, many jobs look interesting on television or in magazines. But remember, you're the one who will be doing the work. Use this checklist against any job possibility:

- What are the training/degree requirements for this line of work?

- What is the best way to enter this field to ensure advancement?

- Which entry-level jobs are best for learning as much as possible?

- Which entry-level jobs are dead ends?

- What is the starting salary for a person in this field?

- Are there extra social/professional obligations that go with this work (unions, professional organization meetings, etc.)?

- What sort of changes are happening in this occupation that will affect future opportunities?

- Who are some people I should talk with to learn more about this career?

- Are there any special considerations for women/men starting in this field?

- Do you need special tools or equipment in this field?

- Are there any occupational hazards in this line of work?

Now, with an idea of the kind of job that appeals to you, the next step is to put yourself in a position to land one—right?

The placement office

You're in luck: Career counseling may be only the first of a two-pronged service your school offers. The second is the placement office, where real jobs are located and offered all the time.

Graduating students, stop-outs and continuing students have always relied on the placement office for help in finding jobs. A good placement office should:

- Offer help in writing a resume.

- Arrange on-campus interviews.

- Help in preparing for interviews (some placement services will even video-tape you in a mock interview situation so that you can see for yourself the kind of impression you make).

• Include a letter of recommendation service. This may be offered for both graduated students and job seekers. It is important to find out how long the letters are kept on file. If they are kept for more than a year or so, you would be wise to take advantage of the service even if you do not intend to use the letters right away. You will not lose anything if you never use them; but if, three years after you graduate, you need letters from two or three professors because you are applying to graduate school, you will be glad that they are on file. Otherwise, you may have a hard time tracking down former professors, reminding them who you are, what you can do, and getting them to write meaningful recommendations.

Ask the secretary for the calendar of organizations, agencies and individuals scheduled to visit the placement office. Target ones you want to interview with.

But wait! At some point, either before you're allowed to schedule an interview, or during an interview itself, you'll have to produce a copy of your resume.

Your resume

Unfortunately, there are a lot of self-proclaimed resume experts around who will help you write what usually turns into a flashy, gimmicky resume that does not really represent you (I've seen them printed on day-glo paper!). Most employers have antennae for these so-called "professionally prepared" resumes and are turned off by them. Resist the temptation to have somebody do it for you and write your own. It isn't all that difficult.

A good resume should be conservative-looking. Avoid exotic typefaces, underlining and decorative graphics—they don't read well. Use at least 12-point type: any smaller is hard to read. Print your resume on white or light beige paper. Blues and grays minimize the contrast between the letters and background. Give interviewers originals, not copies.

As a general rule, your resume should include:

• Your name, address and phone number

• Work experience

• Education

• Honors and awards

Remember, most resume experts agree that you only have about 20 seconds to make an impression. So it's all right to sum up your motives: include a job objective at the top.

Second, tell them what they want to hear. Make your resume reflect the specific skills you're selling: "Managed a staff of 8 and a $100,000 budget." Emphasize hard results: include concrete examples of accomplishments—"Saved 20 percent in labor costs."

Some extras might include your grade point average, professional or personal interests, and membership in professional or community organizations. I could devote an entire chapter to resume-writing but I suggest you read instead:

Your First Resume, 3rd ed. by Ron Fry. Career Press, Inc.

Resumes! Resumes! Resumes! Career Press editors, Career Press, Inc.

The Smart Woman's Guide to Resumes and Job Hunting, 2nd ed. by Julie Adair King and Betsy Sheldon, Career Press, Inc.

Incidentally, information data bases like Nexus (800-828-0422), Connexion (800-338-3282 ext. 561), Job Bank USA (800-296-1872; $30 for 12 months); SkillSearch (800-258-6641; $49 for a year), and HispanData (805-682-5843; $15 for 12 months) for Hispanic professionals, put thousands of resumes at the fingertips of potential employers. Employers specify their criteria for a position, and a random, computer-generated search pulls up the appropriate candidates. Check to see whether your placement office is on-line.

Preparing for interviews

Prepare is the operative word for successful interviews.

First, go to a library or the career resource center and find information and background on the company. Talk to any employees of the company whom you might know; research the company through the local chamber of commerce; and look through professional or trade publications as well as local newspapers to learn about new company development.

Second, anticipate the questions you will be asked. The questions interviewers ask usually fall into two categories—specific questions and sweeping generalizations. The first type is the easier to answer. When an interviewer asks a specific question, "Could you elaborate on your responsibilities at Milne Labs?" you shouldn't have much trouble in answering.

But when an interviewer poses a sweeping generalization such as: "Tell me about yourself," what do you say?

What you *don't* say is, "Well, I was born in Chester, Pennsylvania, in 1951. I have a brother, and I attended school in Philadelphia until I was 15 when my family moved to Edcouch, Texas." You must assume that the interviewer is trying to see how good you are at sorting out what is important from what is unimportant. You answer accordingly, something to the effect that, "Well, I imagine you're most interested in hearing about the aspects of my experience that relate to the opening you have."

Here are some typical questions:

- Why do you want to work for our company?
- What qualifies you for this position?
- What are your personal work strengths and weaknesses?
- Why did you choose our company over others?
- What are your professional goals?

Finally, review your notes on the skills and abilities that you want to emphasize.

When you meet the interviewer, offer a firm handshake; get his or her name correctly—ask the person to repeat it if you didn't catch it—maintain steady eye contact and answer questions as directly as you can. Sincerely thank the interviewer and express your willingness to meet again, if necessary.

Keep in mind that receiving a rejection letter is part of the interviewing process. But you can turn even this into a positive: Follow up by contacting the person who interviewed you. Say that you understand someone else has been hired and ask in what way your qualifications did not suit the particular opening. Ask the interviewer if he or she can make any suggestions about ways you can improve your presentation, further training you might need, other firms that might offer similar openings, etc. Also ask if you may use his or her name in making contacts.

Here are some books to help you with the steps to landing a job:

Getting to the Right Job by S. Cohen and P. deOliveira. Workman Publishing.

101 Great Answers to the Toughest Interview Questions by Ron Fry. Career Press, Inc.

The Smart Woman's Guide to Interviewing and Salary Negotiation by Julie Adair King. Career Press, Inc.

Sweaty Palms: The Neglected Art of Being Interviewed by H.A. Medley. Ten Speed Press.

Work in the New Economy: Careers and Job Seeking into the 21st Century by R. Wegman & M. Johnson. American Association for Counseling and Development.

Your First Interview by Ron Fry. Career Press, Inc.

Getting private help

During your job search, someone might recommend you use a private career counselor.

Choose one carefully. Here are some tips:

- Select a counselor with a good reputation in career counseling.
- Check to see whether the counselor is licensed or board certified: a licensed professional counselor (licensed by your state), a National Board Certified Counselor (NBCC), or a National Certified Career Counselor (NCC).
- Talk with former clients of the counselor to obtain their recommendations.

A career counselor cannot and should not:

- Tell you what to major in so that you will be sure to get a job when you graduate.
- Suggest some careers for you.
- Tell you which careers will be "good" in the future.

The good news is a career counselor can provide objectivity not always available with family, friends and peers. A career counselor typically possesses a variety of facilitative "tools" that may aid in decision-making. You should seek career counseling if you become significantly uncomfortable in trying to make an occupational choice or, if for any reason, you are unable to resolve the indecision independently.

Doing some legwork on your own

However, there are many ways to deal with career indecision prior or in addition to seeking career counseling. Teachers, parents and friends can be excellent sources of information about careers, for example.

Try these methods:

- *Brainstorming*. This works well with help from someone such as your spouse, friend or parent.

- *Calling friends.* Remember that 65 percent of all job vacancies are never advertised. And the preferred source of job candidates among employers is word-of-mouth referrals from a trusted source who knows the candidate well.

- *Library.* Read over professional magazines, even ones that do not seem to be immediately relevant. Remember, you are skimming them for ideas.

- *Sunday newspapers.* Read the help-wanted ads and remember that an ad in the newspaper is usually for several positions. Even if you are under- or over-qualified, that company or organization may have a job for you. Read the want ads not so much for job openings as for ideas.

- *Yellow pages / White pages.* Use them for ideas—25 percent of ideas for job leads come from here.

- *Industrial and professional directories.* Pick up some directories and read over the table of contents, study job titles and work titles; think of the best access to a job in the company. Use directories such as: *U.S. Government Handbook, Directory of Associations, Standard and Poor's, Moody's Industrial Directory, Ward's Business Directory of U.S. Private and Public Companies, The Corporate Directory of U.S. Public Companies, Best's Insurance Reports, Polk's Bank Directory,* and *Corptech's Corporate Technology Directory.*

Consider joining and becoming active in your college's alumni association for an excellent source of entree into a wide variety of businesses and professional organizations.

Don't forget to use your professors as contacts. Many of them are contacted by employers who are looking for talent in various fields.

Professional fraternities and associations can also be a rich source of contacts and job leads. After all, you can assume that most of the members are already employed in the field of your interest.

Employment agencies: Proceed with caution

When it comes to mailing out your resume, turning up job leads and so on, you may be tempted just to take your campaign to a commercial employment agency and let them do the work for you.

Well, let's be blunt: Commercial agencies are not in business to help you find the right job—that's up to you. They are in business to make money for themselves. This can sometimes mean placing you in any job that comes along. Hey, don't complain: You wanted a job—they found you a job.

Also, the fee you will be charged is not small—10 percent of the first year's salary (payable upon employment) is generally the standard minimum. The fee goes up on higher paying jobs—generally 15 percent plus one-half percent per $1,000 over $15,000 on jobs that pay more than $10,000 a year. Of course, if you should happen to be broke at the time of employment, a bank loan at regular interest rates can be arranged to cover the fee!

There are times when the use of a commercial agency is justified. If you have a special skill, for instance, it's worthwhile to use an agency that specializes in jobs of that type, especially if most of the jobs are fee-paid—meaning the hiring company pays the agency's fee. There are agencies that specialize in teachers, engineers, health related positions, etc.

Just keep these points in mind:

- Be skeptical about classified ads the agencies place in newspapers. Choose an agency by asking around and getting advice from the Better Business Bureau and consumer protection agencies.

- Don't sign anything until you fully understand the terms. You may be agreeing to accept every interview the agency sets up for you.

- Understand the salary arrangement on the particular job before going on the interview.

- Don't tell your counselor what other jobs you are applying for. If you do, the agency may send other applicants to compete against you for the position. (Hard to believe, isn't it?)

- Don't put yourself in the "counselor's hands" and expect that he or she will work things out. Continue to job-hunt on your own.

- Some agencies have such terrible reputations with the business community that they will send you on interviews while suggesting that you not admit to the hiring company who sent you. This should be your cue to sever all connections with that agency.

Personnel agencies are one more source of leads in the job-hunt, but when using an agency, be aware and be skeptical. Use the agency; don't let the agency use you.

Choosing between job offers

A go-getter like youself might wind up in a very happy circumstance: having more than one job to choose from. What should you consider?

All you need to do is compare job offers on a point-by-point basis. In other words, weigh:

- Salary, of course. But this is only one criteria.

- Benefits, such as insurance policies, hospitalization, access to a credit union, bonuses, annual physical examinations, educational benefits.

- Atmosphere.

- Location (and the likelihood of relocation at some point).

- Working conditions.

- Opportunities for advancement.

- People you'll be working with. There's a good saying to keep in mind: "You can only be as good as the people you work with."

Interview
How to increase your marketability

Craig Kopstain, assistant director of placement at Northwestern University in Evanston, Illinois, said it's a big mistake for students not to put their career placement center to full use.

"Anybody who has access to one and doesn't use it passes up an immense opportunity," Kopstain said. "If a school doesn't have a placement center, the students ought at least to talk to a career counselor or alumni organization."

Kopstain said placement directors are like brokers. They're brokering for the student and for the businesses they communicate with.

"I work the system both ways," Kopstain said. "I'm a consultant for businesses and students."

Kopstain said Northwestern has a full-service operation career placement center. Students who are registered with the center enjoy a variety of services.

"We have articles and ads in the paper, fliers—and we're listed in a computer data base that's available to all students," Kopstain said. "I advise all students to participate."

"It's one of the rites of seniorhood at Northwestern," Kopstain continued. "All seniors know when they return to campus their senior year that they have to touch base with the career placement center."

Kopstain said Northwestern's career placement office, which began in the late 1930s, is one of the oldest in the country. He said this center and similar offices at other colleges make all the difference in the marketability of graduating seniors.

"If you want to be a hot target for businesses, in addition to a high grade point average you need three other things," Kopstain said. "These are communication skills, leadership skills and internship or co-op work experience."

"Our game plan for Northwestern students is to get them sophisticated on how to interview, how to present themselves and how to assess the businesses they contact," Kopstain continued. "It makes all the difference to them."

In addition to on-campus recruiting, Northwestern's career placement office has a separate, continually updated listing of 2,000 to 4,000 other job opportunities available to students.

The University also has an alumni network of several thousand people who inform seniors and graduate students of their work experiences. These are resource people who have information to offer, not jobs.

Also included in Northwestern is a computerized program called Career Search. Its data base contains 380,000 employers from all over the country.

The University also offers presentations on long-distance job searches, interviewing techniques and other job-related topics. A library of 300 video tapes on such topics is also available.

Kopstain said Northwestern's Student Advisory Board is extremely active in career placement activities. He said the board members include presidents of some good-sized organizations—The Society of Women Engineers, National Society of Black Engineers, and Tau Beta Pi, to name a few.

Students from the board, with Kopstain as their adviser, met with 25 companies in the 1993-94 school year alone. Anytime these students meet with a company, they have to write a paper and present it to their organizations, Kopstain said.

"Our goal is to prepare students early on," Kopstain said. "A typical senior at Northwestern can get 10 to 12 interviews per month."

Advice for adult students changing careers

- "Take the transition process with a grain of salt. Don't think your life is ending. It's basically just beginning."

- "Interviews are just conversations, and people are friendlier than you think."

- "Take risks and concentrate on team effort and quality because those are the basic expectations of employers. You must have that to compete in the world of work today."

- "Put your fears away. Leave them at home when you go to interview."

- "Be prepared to learn and keep learning throughout the rest of your career."

- "Don't be afraid of change. Look forward to it. It will keep you young, and new, and thinking, and challenged."

Chapter 8

How Will I Keep My Education Current?

You've heard those statistics about how rapidly the amount of information is growing: The last I heard was that it doubles every 10 years.

No one can keep up—or needs to—with this torrent of facts, but to stay on the cutting edge of your field, you do need to commit to one thing: lifelong learning.

When my grandfather was a streetcar conductor in the early part of this century, everything he learned through the eighth grade put him in good stead his entire life. My mother, on the other hand, used her high school education to further her understanding: She is comfortable in libraries, finding books and articles that interest her. Fifteen years ago, I thought a master's degree was all I would need to manage a good teaching career. But I found that additional schooling became necessary after all.

In the same way, to be effective—respected, actually—keeping up with developments in your field will be very important. Here are ways to keep your education polished and bright by maintaining it. First, other people have a lot they can share with you.

Build a professional network

You might feel shy about contacting specialists in a field, but in fact many experts are interested in what is happening in their professional field—you bring fresh news! These contacts are potentially beneficial to both you and the professional.

The first place to start in developing a network is with your adviser and other faculty members in the department in which you're studying. Make appointments with them individually to record the names and addresses of people they feel are doing work that would be of interest to you. While meeting with your adviser and faculty members, ask them to recommend the names of professional organizations and journals that they feel will be most helpful to you.

Professional meetings and journals are another excellent way to meet and discuss topics of special importance to you. Most departments strongly encourage students to participate in professional organizations and will often arrange for group transportation and lodging at a lower cost.

Write to the professional organizations you identify and request information on their publications, membership fees and local chapters. It is well worth the investment.

Finally, networking at large is very valuable. Networking is planning: making contacts and sharing information for professional and personal gain. To build an effective network, an individual needs both formal and informal networks in place. Formal networks are the type you can actually join, usually with dues and regular meetings. These could include an entrepreneur association, a civic group or an alumnae association. Informal net-works consist of people more loosely tied together, such as friends, colleagues or people you meet at a ball game. A good network contains both types.

Be on the lookout for people to include in your network, and networks to join. Here are some steps for building your network:

- Set your goals. Decide who you want in your network and how you'll contact them. Maybe you'll concentrate on joining organizations. Make lists of names. Add them to your rolodex.

- Take action. Reserve special networking time, say 3 to 5 p.m. on Tuesdays, if your schedule allows. When attending meetings, set a goal of a certain number of new people to meet.

- Practice network etiquette: Respect contacts' names. Get an okay before you use a person's name as a referral to reach someone else. Call people at times that are convenient for them. Follow through on promises: that article you mentioned, that phone number you said you'd provide. Invite people to lunch, send holiday cards, clip articles of interest to your contacts. Thank everyone who helps.

Here's a book that's just about effective networking:

Network Your Way to Job and Career Success: Your Complete Guide to Creating New Opportunities by R. Krannich & C. Krannich. 1989. Impact Publications.

Interview for information

There will undoubtedly be persons who are key players in your field whom you'd like to meet, but don't know personally.

Send a short, personalized letter to your contact to request an interview. This is a well-known practice: it's called interviewing for information.

In your letter you should abide by these courtesies:

- Include a cordial personal statement that links you to the person somehow: a mutual acquaintance, an article you read, etc.

- Don't pressure the person by asking for a job.

- Get to the point: Indicate you are requesting assistance to learn more about an occupation or organization.

- Close the letter by requesting an appointment and indicating you will call for a convenient time.

Then, make a follow-up call: Ask for the appointment.

Prepare for your conversation by learning about the organization and its industry and by developing a list of specific questions. During your meeting, be organized—respect the person's time; ask for advice about your career plans; request referrals to others; leave a copy of your resume. However, don't ask for a job—it will be interpreted as an ambush. After all, you said you were just shopping for information: now you put the arm on the person for a position. It's not classy.

And speaking of being classy, don't forget to send a thank-you note.

Make reading a habit

Americans have a big appetite for information. Consequently, whatever field you're in, there's a publication carrying regular information about new developments. Consider, for instance:

- Newspapers
- Weekly news magazines: *U.S. News & World Report, Business Week*
- Monthly magazines: *Fortune, Money*
- Business sections of newspapers
- In-house papers and newsletters for corporate employees
- Chamber of commerce publications
- Local magazines
- Professional and trade journals
- Civil service offices
- *The Occupational Outlook Handbook and CIS Occupational Information*

Now, let's get a little more specific.

For a general understanding of business, *The Wall Street Journal* is the most widely read daily newspaper. In addition to be-ing the basic news source about business, the *Journal* has become recognized as one of the most well-written newspapers in the nation.

Forbes, Fortune and *Business Week* are the country's leading business magazines. Each tries to "scoop" its competitors and provide more useful information. America's interest in business has led to the creation of many other fine periodicals, including *Investors Daily, Inc.* and *Financial World.* Some industries have even attracted their own business magazines to cover them.

Major national dailies are must-reads for workers who want to stay on top: newspapers like *The New York Times, Chicago Tribune, The Los Angeles Times* and *The Washington Post* are well-known for their coverage of local, national and international business developments.

In addition to these sources, there are a multitude of general business directories. The best-known include *Ward's Business Directory of U.S. Private and Public Companies; Standard & Poor's Register of Corporations, Directors and Executives;* and *The Corporate Directory of U.S. Public Companies.* These directories are updated annually and provide basic information on thousands of public and private companies.

There are also directories available on specific industries and topics. These include *Best's Insurance Reports, Polk's Bank Directory* and *Corptech's Corporate Technology Directory.*

For basic statistics on American business, there is no finer book than the *Statistical Abstract of the United States.* It is published annually by the Government Printing Office and is available in almost all libraries and at Government Printing Office bookstores for $32 trade paper, or $38 hardback.

Use high-tech assists

Almost all of the sources mentioned (and many more) are available in electronic format: usually in more than one. The directories are almost all available on CD-ROM discs. Periodicals and newspapers are also all available on-line.

On-line sources are available to any individual who has a computer and a modem. Dow Jones News Retrieval (800-522-3567), Mead's LEXIS/ NEXIS (800-227-4908) and Knight-Ridder's DIALOG (800-334-2564) are for general business research. However, they are ex-pensive, costing as much as several dollars per minute of use. One search for company information can easily cost hundreds of dollars.

CD-ROM technology allows the contents of dozens of books, or hundreds of periodicals, to be stored on a single optical disk. UMI's ABI/INFORM and Courier Plus CD-ROMs allow you to scan summaries of 25 newspapers and 800 periodicals (going back several years) for articles of interest. Disclosure (800-843-7747), Standard & Poor's (800-525-8640), Silver Platter Information (800-343-5414) have CD-ROM products containing summary or full-text annual reports and financial data for thousands of companies.

While costly to purchase (prices for these products can run from a few thousand to tens of thousands of dollars) and requiring a PC and CD-ROM drive, most of these CD-ROMs are available in libraries.

If you have access to a fax machine, still other services await you. *Dow Jones*, *The Economist* and other periodicals are developing services that allow users to dial a 900 number and request topical reprints or business reports using a touch-tone phone and a code published in their periodicals. The document is delivered in seconds by fax. *Dow Jones' Facts Delivered* allows you to order company reports by calling 800-445-9454. Reports are promptly delivered by fax or mail. *Fortune Business Reports* has a similar service (800-989-4636) that provides reports containing general backgound information on the company and up-to-minute news from the Reuters wire service. It is available by fax or mail.

Keep up on the job market

Sure, you have a job, but keep your eyes open. As British Prime Minister Benjamin Disreali said, "The secret to success is being ready for your opportunity when it comes."

Hoover's MasterList of Major U.S. Companies 1994—one of the best-known annual directories in the country—provides information about hiring trends at America's biggest companies; *Chicago Tribune* columnist Carol Kleiman's *100 Best Jobs for the 1990s & Beyond* provides good advice about the changing employment climate; and America OnLine's *Career Center* includes a wide variety of information about employment opportunities. See Appendix 3, too, for more good titles in the career planning field.

Watch or listen to quality programs

Even if your electronic repertoire is limited to cable TV, you can watch "Wall Street Week," the "Nightly Business Report," CNBC and other worthwhile business programming. Most National Public Radio affiliates also carry an excellent business program called "Marketplace."

Interview
'Benchmarking' to stay current

Bruce Rismiller, former vice president of Carson Pirie Scott & Co. is the recently retired executive vice president of Northwest Airlines. At the airlines he was also the chief quality officer and was responsible for human resources and labor.

According to Rismiller, the best way to keep up-to-date in any field is to observe what others in that field are doing. This process of learning about your job by reading about what others are doing and by interviewing and observing others in a similar field is called *benchmarking*.

"Benchmarking is the most important way there is to stay current in the job place," Rismiller said.

As vice president of Carson Pirie Scott, Rismiller said he sent his communications specialist out to benchmark what communications processes other businesses had intact. "We found out Xerox had the best communications, so we met the people at Xerox, determined what processes would fit in at Carson and took the best of their experiences," he said.

However, benchmarking concentrates on studying other people's work processes. Rismiller said it's equally important for every individual in any business to monitor his or her own performance.

This is done by talking to the people who are affected by this performance—the customers. Through interviewing customers or issuing surveys, individuals can receive feedback about their work performance.

"At Pontiac when someone buys a new car, a worker calls the new owner up that night and says, 'I understand you bought a car that I built—how do you like it,' " Rismiller said. "In this manner, the worker gets instant feedback on his work performance."

Rismiller also worked with Professor Tom Roach from Purdue University to set up intern programs at Northwest Airlines. "I feel the first job assignment, if done well, can set a person on one heck of a career path," he said.

"In every training program we had, those interns were rubbing shoulders with people who had a lot more experience," Rismiller said. "After a while, the students were acting the way professional business people with a lot of experience would act."

Rismiller said it's also important to read trade journals and other publications in order to stay current in any field. He also recommended accessing information through computer data bases.

"If you have a fax machine and a computer, you're there," Rismiller said. "Data bases are sometimes part of associations, libraries and colleges, and they're definitely accessible."

Tips on staying current

- Put yourself in situations where you can learn.
- "Walk the walk" and "talk of the talk" of the people in positions you aspire to.
- Talk with the people affected by a worker's performance: your endpoint is to learn what satisfies customers.
- Volunteer to find out answers to questions, even if you haven't a clue at first. It's a small risk, but it will put you on the cutting edge. Seek out those opportunities.

Abbreviations of Degrees

Undergraduate Degrees

A.A.	Associate in Arts
A.A.S.	Associate in Applied Science
A.S.	Associate in Science
B.A.	Bachelor of Arts
B.S.	Bachelor of Science
B.B.A.	Bachelor of Business Administration
B.E.	Bachelor of Engineering
B.Ed.	Bachelor of Education
B.F.A.	Bachelor of Fine Arts
B.P.S.	Bachelor of Professional Studies
B.Tech.	Bachelor of Technology

Graduate Academic Degrees

M.A.	Master of Arts
M.S.	Master of Science
M. Phil.	Master of Philosophy
Ph.D.	Doctor of Philosophy

Graduate Professional Degrees

M.Arch.	Master of Architecture
M.A.T.	Master of Arts in Teaching
M.B.A.	Master of Business Administration
M.Ed.	Master of Education
M.F.A.	Master of Fine Arts
M.L.S.	Master of Library Science
M.P.A.	Master of Public Administration
M.S.	Master of Science
M.S.W.	Master of Social Work
D.D.S.	Doctor of Dental Surgery
Ed.D.	Doctor of Education
J.D.	Doctor of Law
M.D.	Doctor of Medicine
D.V.M.	Doctor of Veterinary Medicine

Advice for Learning Disabled Adults

Stevie Wonder said, "A handicap is not a handicap unless you make it one."

This also seems to be the implication of federal laws regarding differently abled students and educational institutions.

Section 504 of the Rehabilitation Act of 1973 effectively bars discrimination in areas of recruitment, hiring and classification of individuals by any institution receiving federal funds. For students with learning disabilities, this act prohibits colleges and universities from denying them admission solely because they have a learning disability but otherwise meet the school's established admission criteria. The law insures that the doors of higher education will not be shut on students merely because they have a disability.

However, not all schools with programs for students with learning disabilities use the same definition of "learning disability" beyond that contained in P.L. 94-142. For instance, some schools accept students with a broader range of learning deficits into their learning disabilites program than others.

On the other hand, even if students with learning disabilities qualify for a "most selective" or "highly selective" schools, they may nonetheless choose a less competitive college or university that has a more comprehensive program where they will benefit from more direct assistance and remedial or tutorial programs.

A comprehensive program for learning disabled students will include diagnostic and prescriptive planning, advisement, counseling, remediation, tutoring, special courses and a range of auxiliary aids and services. The key to such a program is that its components are provided in a manner specifically designed to meet the needs of students with a learning disability, and that it is staffed with personnel with appropriate training and experience.

Generally, students whose learning disabilities were diagnosed early and who spent much of their school career in special programs or classes for the learning disabled might need a comprehensive program, while students who were successful in regular high school classes with some outside assistance might find special services enough.

Frequently, special courses are offered for adult students who are learning disabled. These courses provide the prerequisite skills and social and emotional support necessary for such students to suceed in college. They may be credit or noncredit courses and may or may not count in a student's overall grade point average. Examples of special courses are:

- Developmental reading
- English composition
- Fundamentals of communication
- Language remediation
- Study skills
- Note-taking techniques
- Writing research papers
- Speed writing
- Typing
- Word processing
- Memory improvement

- Personal psychology
- College survival

In addition, comprehensive programs also provide a number of auxiliary aids and services to help students with learning disabilities compensate:

Tape recordings and taped textbooks. Learning disabled students often have difficulty taking notes from class lectures. The tape recorder becomes a valuable auxiliary aid for them. They are able to tape-record a lecture at the same time they take notes. Later, they can replay the tapes to check their notes for completeness and accuracy. The use of a tape recorder reduces the heavy demands upon their auditory memory, language processing and writing skills. Because of the value of tape recorders, professors are encouraged to allow students with learning disabilities to use them in their classes.

Note-takers. Typically, note-takers are students. They have been identified as good note-takers who are reliable, competent in the subject, and have legible handwriting. A duplicate set of notes is given to the student who is learning diabled. Usually the note-taker does not know the identity of the student receiving the notes.

Alternative arrangements. Often, students with a learning disability have difficulty completing a test within a specified time limit, accurately reading test questions and writing answers. Arrangements are made with professors to allow students to take course examinations with one of the number of alternatives:

- Extended time limits
- Questions dictated onto an audio tape
- Questions read by a proctor
- Responses dictated to a proctor
- Responses dictated onto audio tapes

- Responses typed rather than handwritten
- Questions presented in a different format, such as multiple choice in place of essay
- Take-home examinations or projects in place of written examinations.

College staff members often serve as advocates for learning disabled students. Check with the office of student affairs or the admissions office for more information.

Appendix 3

Resource List

Recommended books and publications

College Choice

Barron's Top Fifty: An Inside Look at America's Top Colleges. Fischgrund, Tom, ed., Barron's.

Choosing a College. Miller, G.P. College Entrance Examination Board.

College Applications & Essays: A How-To Handbook. Van Raalte, Susan D., Arco Publishing.

College, Getting In and Staying In. Lockerbie, D. Bruce. Eerdmans Publishing.

College Match: A Blueprint for Choosing the School That's Best for You. Antonoff, Steven R., Octameron.

Colleges With Programs for Students With Learning Disabilities. Peterson's Guides.

Profiles of American Colleges: Index of College Majors. Barron's Educational Series, Inc.

The Ultimate College Shopper's Guide. Evans, Heather and Sullivan, Deidre. Addison-Wesley.

College Costs

Bear's Guide to Finding Money for College. Bear, John. Ten Speed Press.

College Loans From Uncle Sam: The Borrower's Guide That Explains It All. Leider, Anna, ed., Octameron.

College Student's Handbook to Financial Assistance & Planning. Cook, Melissa L., Moonbeam Publications.

The Consumer Guide to College Funding. United Resource Press.

Cutting College Costs. Duffy, James P., Career Press.

Financial Aid Report With the Directory of Private Scholarships & Grants. Perpetual Progress Media.

Free Money for College From the Government. Blum, Laurie. H., Holt & Co.

Graduate Scholarship Directory: The Complete Guide to Scholarships, Fellowships, Grants & Loans for Graduate and Professional Study (3rd Ed.), Cassidy, Daniel J., Career Press.

The Great American National Scholarships & Grants Guide. Darby, Anthony. DCLAREN Publishing.

How to Go to College for Free. Bowman, Linda. Probus Publishing Co.

How to Send Your Kid or Yourself to College Almost for Free. McKee, Cynthia R. & McKee, Phillip C., Jr. Hearst Books.

International Scholarship Directory: The Complete Guide to Financial Aid for Study Anywhere in the World (3rd Ed.), Cassidy, Daniel J., Career Press.

Keys to Financing a College Education. Dennis, Marguerite J., Barrons.

Paying Less for College, Peterson's.

Princeton Review: The Student Access Financial Aid & Planning System. Martz, Geoffrey. Random House.

Scholarships, Fellowships & Loans, Gale Research.

Selected Information Resources on Scholarships, Fellowships & Grants. Gordon Press.

Careers

Career Actualization and Life Planning. Blocher, D.H., Love Publishing.

Career Planning & Development for College Students and Recent Graduates. Steele, J.E. and Morgan, M.S., NTC Publishing Group.

Career Satisfaction and Success: How to Know and Manage Your Strengths. Haldane, B., Wellness Behavior.

Careers: Exploration and Decision. Rettig, J.L. Davis S., Lake Publishers.

Career Tracks. Schwartz, L. and Brechner, I., Ballantine Books.

Choosing a Career in Business. Stumpf, S.A., Simon & Schuster.

Coming Alive From Nine to Five. Michelozzi, B., Mayfield.

Exploring Careers: The ASVAB Student Workbook. U.S. Department of Defense (available free to anyone taking the Armed Services Vocational Aptitude Battery).

New Horizons: The Education and Career Planning Guide for Adults. Haponski, W. C. and McCabe, C.E., Peterson's.

The Occupational Outlook Handbook, U.S. Department of Labor.

Part-Time Careers: For Anyone Who Wants More Than Just a Job—But Less Than a 40-Hour Week!, Joyce Hadley, Career Press.

Successful Recareering: When Changing Jobs Isn't Enough, Joyce Schwarz, Career Press.

What Color is Your Parachute? Bolles, R.N., Ten Speed Press.

Where the Jobs Are: America's Hottest Careers for the 90s, Mark Satterfield, Career Press.

College level tests

ACT: The American College Testing Program. Levy, Norman, Ph.D. and Levy, Joan U., Ph.D., Arco.

Official Handbook for the CLEP Examinations. College Board Staff. College Board.

The Princeton Review—Cracking the System: The SAT and PSAT. Robinson, Adam. Random House.

Remember to Read the Question: A Thinking Student's Guide to the SAT & Beyond. Morrison, et al., Kendall-Hunt.

Ten SATs. College Board.

Career development

The Black Manager: Making It in the Corporate World. Dickens, Floyd, Jr. & Dickens, Jacqueline B., AMACOM.

Childhood Dreams—Career Answers: A Woman's Practical & Playful Guide to the Career Puzzle. Chaney, Marti and Thayer, Vicki. LifeWorks Press.

The Complete Job & Career Handbook: One Hundred One Ways to Get from Here to There. Feingold, S. Norman and Feingold, Marilyn N., Garrett Park.

How to Locate Jobs & Land Interviews. French, Al. Career Press.

Starting Over: You in the New Workplace. Danna, Jo. Palomino Press.

Temp By Choice: The Complete Guide to Successful Temporary Employment, Thrailkill, Diane. Career Press.

Your Own Worst Enemy: How to Overcome Career Self-Sabotage. DuBrin, Andrew J., AMACOM.

Women

Dual-Career Families. Sekaran, U., Jossey-Bass.

Hard Choices: How Women Decide About Work, Career, and Motherhood. Gerson, K., University of California Press.

How to Find Money for College: The Woman Student. Schwartz, Saryl Z., Path-College.

Science for Girls. Kelly, Allison. Taylor & Francis.

Sharing It All: The Rewards and Struggles of Two-Career Families. Gilbert, L.A., Plenum.

The Smart Woman's Guide to Resumes and Job Hunting, 2nd Ed., King, Julie A. and Sheldon, Betsy. Career Press.

The Young Women's Guide to Better SAT Scores: Fighting the Gender Trap. Kelly-Benjamin, Kathleen. Bantam.

Addresses, organizations & books you can use

If you're considering going in the trades, chances are apprenticeship programs are offered in your area, probably at the local community college. Check with the offices listed for more information.

State Offices, Bureau of Apprenticeship and Training

Alabama
Berry Building, Suite 102
2017 Second Avenue, North
Birmingham, AL 35203
205-731-1308

Alaska
Federal Building and Courthouse
222 West 7th Street, Room 554
Anchorage, AK 99513
907-271-5035

Arizona
3221 N. Sixteenth St., Suite 302
Phoenix, AZ 85016
602-640-2964

Arkansas
Federal Building, Room 3507
700 West Capitol Street
Little Rock, AR 72201
501-324-5415

California
211 Main Street, Room 350
San Francisco, CA 94105-1978
415-744-6581

Colorado
U.S. Custom House, Room 480
721 Nineteenth Street
Denver, CO 80202
303-844-4793

Connecticut
Federal Building, Room 367
135 High Street
Hartford, CT 06103
203-240-4311

Delaware
Federal Building, Lock Box 36
844 King Street
Wilmington, DE 19801
302-573-6113

Florida
City Center Building, Suite 5117
227 North Bronough Street
Tallahassee, FL 32301
904-681-7161

Georgia
1371 Peachtree St., NE, Room 418
Atlanta, GA 30367
404-347-4403

Hawaii
300 Ala Moana Blvd., Room 5113
P.O. Box 50203
Honolulu, HI 96850
808-541-2518

Idaho
3050 N. Lake Harbor La., Ste. 128
P.O. Box 006
Boise, ID 83703
208-334-1013

Illinois
230 S. Dearborn St., Room 758
Chicago, IL 60604
312-353-4690

Indiana
Federal Building and U.S.
   Courthouse, Room 414
46 East Ohio Street
Indianapolis, IN 46204
317-226-7592

Iowa
Federal Building, Room 715
210 Walnut Street
Des Moines, IA 50309
515-284-4690

Kansas
Federal Building, Room 256
444 S.E. Quincy Street
Topeka, KS 66683-3571
913-295-2624

Kentucky
Federal Building, Room 187-J
600 Federal Place
Louisville, KY 40202
502-582-5223

Louisiana
3535 South Sherwood Forest Blvd.
Baton Rouge, LA 70816
504-389-0263

Maine
Federal Building, Room 408-B
68 Sewall Street, P.O. Box 917
Augusta, ME 04330
207-622-8235

Maryland
Charles Center, Room 1028
Federal Building
31 Hopkins Plaza
Baltimore, MD 21201
410-962-2676

Massachusetts
One Congress Street, 11th Fl.
Boston, MA 02114
617-565-2291

Michigan
Federal Building, Room 304
801 South Waverly
Lansing, MI 48917
517-377-1640

Minnesota
Federal Building and U.S.
    Courthouse, Room 134
316 Robert Street
St. Paul, MN 55101
612-290-3951

Mississippi
Federal Building, Suite 1010
100 West Capitol Street
Jackson, MS 39269
601-965-4346

Missouri
122 Spruce Street, 9102E
St. Louis, MO 63103
314-539-2522

Montana
Federal Office Building, Room 394
Drawer 10055
301 South Park Avenue
Helena, MT 59626-0055
406-449-5261

Nebraska
106 South Fifteenth St., Room 801
Omaha, NE 68102
402-221-3281

Nevada
Post Office Building, Room 311
301 E. Stewardt Ave, Box 1987
Las Vegas, NV 89101
702-388-6397

New Hampshire
143 North Main Street
Concord, NH 03301
603-225-1444

New Jersey
Parkway Towers-Bldg. E
485-Route #1
South Iselin, NJ 08830
908-750-9191

New Mexico
505 Marquette, Room 830
Albuquerque, NM 87102
505-766-2398

New York
Federal Building, Room 810
North Pearl and Clinton Avenues
Albany, NY 12202
518-472-4800

North Carolina
4407 Bland Road, Suite 350
Raleigh, NC 27609
919-790-2801

North Dakota
New Federal Building, Room 428
653 Second Avenue, North
Fargo, ND 58102
701-239-5415

Ohio
200 North High Street
Room 605
Columbus, OH 43215
614-469-7375

Oklahoma
51 Yale Building, Room 305
5110 South Yale
Tulsa, OK 74135
918-581-7412

Oregon
Federal Building, #526
1220 SW Third Avenue
Portland, OR 97204
503-326-3157

Pennsylvania
Federal Building, Room 773
228 Walnut Street
Harrisburg, PA 17108
717-782-3496

Rhode Island
100 Hartford Avenue
Providence, RI 02909
401-528-5198

South Carolina
Strom Thurmond Federal Bldg.
1835 Assembly Street
Room 838
Columbia, SC 29201
803-765-5547

South Dakota
Court House Plaza
Room 107
300 North Dakota Avenue
Sioux Falls, SD 57102
605-330-4326

Tennessee
460 Metroplex Drive
Suite 101-A
Nashville, TN 37211
615-781-5318

Texas
VA Building, Room 2102
2320 LeBranch Street
Houston, TX 77004
713-750-1696

Utah
1745 West 1700 South, Room 1051
Salt Lake City, UT 84104
801-524-5700

Vermont
96 College St., Suite 103
Burlington, VT 05401
802-951-6278

Virginia
400 N. Eighth St., Room 10-020
Richmond, VA 23240
804-771-2488

Washington
1111 Third Avenue, Room 950
Seattle, WA 98101-3212
206-442-4756

West Virginia
1 Dunbar Plaza
Suite E
Dunbar, WV 25064
304-293-5314

Wisconsin
Federal Center, Room 303
212 East Washington Avenue
Madison, WI 53703
608-264-5377

Wyoming
J.C. O'Mahoney Federal Center
2120 Capitol Avenue
Room 5013
P.O. Box 1126
Cheyenne, WY 82001
307-772-2448 Ext. 2448

Short Residency or No Residency Degree Programs

You're not limited to attending a college or university in your area. The following institutions require that students spend a minimal amount of time on campus—just a summer, for example. Requirements will vary, so contact the college or university directly.

The American College
270 Bryn Mawr Avenue
Bryn Mawr, PA 19910

American Open University of
    New York
Institute of Technology
Central Islip, NY 11722

Antioch University
School for Adult & Experiential
    Learning
Yellow Springs, OH 45387

Atlantic Union College
Adult Degree Program (ADP)
South Lancaster, MA 01561

Bemidji State University
Center for Extended Learning
1500 Birchmont Drive NE
Bemidji, MN 56601

Berean College of the Assemblies
    of God
1445 Boonville Avenue
Springfield, MO 65802

Bradley University
Division of Continuing Education
and Professional Development
Heitz Hall, Lower Level
Peoria, IL 61625

Brigham Young University
Degrees by Independent Study
305 Harman Building
Provo, UT 84602

Burlington College
Director of Admissions
95 North Avenue
Burlington, VT 05401

Caldwell College
9 Ryerson Avenue
Caldwell, NJ 07006

California College for Health
Sciences
Center for Degree Studies
222 West 24th Street
National City, CA 91950

California State University/
Domingues Hills
HUX M. A. Program
Sac 2/Room 2126
Carson, CA 90747

Central Michigan University
Extended Degree Programs
Rowe Hall 130
Mount Pleasant, MI 48859

Charter Oak College
The Exchange, Suite 171
270 Farmington Avenue
Farmington, CT 06032

City University
16661 Northup Way
Bellevue, WA 98008

Colorado State University
Colorado SURGE
Division of Continuing Education-
Spruce Hall
Fort Collins, CO 80523

Columbia Union College
Department of External Programs
7600 Flower Avenue
Takoma Park, MD 20912

Eckerd College
Program for Experienced
Learners (PEL)
4500 54th Avenue South
St. Petersburg, FL 33711

The Electronic University
Network
CompuLearning Systems, Inc.
245 Northpoint Street, Suite 409
San Francisco, CA 94133

Elizabethtown College
Center for Continuing Education
EXCEL Program
One Alpha Drive
Elizabethtown, PA 17022

Embry-Riddle Aeronautical
University
Department of Independent
Studies
Daytona Beach, FL 32114

Empire State College/State
University of New York
1 Union Avenue
Saratoga Springs, NY 12866

Ferris State University
Gerholz Institute for Lifelong
   Learning
226 Alumni Building
901 South State Street
Big Rapids, MI 49307

The Fielding Institute
2112 Santa Barbara Street
Santa Barbara, CA 93105

Goddard College
Plainfield, VT 05667

Grantham College of Engineering
34641 Grantham College Road
P.O. Box 5700
Slidell, LA 70469

Griggs University
Collegiate Division of Home Study
   International
P.O. Box 4437
Silver Spring, MD 20914

Indiana Institute of Technology
Extended Studies Program
1600 East Washington Boulevard
Ft. Wayne, IN 46803

Indiana University
External Degree Program
Student Union Building
   Room 526
620 Union Drive
Indianapolis, IN 46202

Iowa State University
Off-Campus Programs
College of Agriculture
Ames, IA 50011

Johnston State College
External Degree Program
Johnson, VT 05656

Judson College
Adult Degree Program
Marion, AL 36756

Kansas State University
Non-Traditional Study Program
Division of Continuing Education
College Court Building
Manhattan, KS 66506

Lesley College
29 Everett Street
Cambridge, MA 02138

Liberty University
School of LifeLong Learning
P.O. Box 11803
Lynchburg, VA 24506

Lindenwood College
209 south Kingshighway
St. Charles, MO 63301

Loma Linda University
School of Public Health, Extended
   Program
Nichol Hall 1706
Loma Linda, CA 92354

Loyola University
Loyola's Institute for Ministry
   Extension Program
Box 67, 6363 St. Charles Avenue
New Orleans, LA 70118

Mary Baldwin College
Adult Degree Program
Staunton, VA 24401

rywood College
f-Campus Degree Program
Undergraduate School
2300 Adams Avenue
Scranton, PA 18509

Metropolitan State University
Suite 121, Metro Square
121 Seventh Place East
St. Paul, MN 55101

Mind Extension University
(ME/U)
The Education Network
9697 East Mineral Avenue
Englewood, CO 80112

Murray State University
Bachelor of Independent Studies
Center for Continuing
Education/Academic Outreach
Murray, KY 42071

New College of Hofstra University
University Without Walls at New
College
Hempstead, NY 11550

Northwood Institute
External Plan of Study
3225 Cook Road
Midland, MI 48640

Nova University
3301 College Avenue
Fort Lauderdale, FL 33314

Ohio University
Adult Learning Services
301 Tupper Hall
Athens, OH 45701

Oklahoma City University
Competency-Based Degree
Program (CBDP)
2501 North Blackwelder
Oklahoma City, OK 73106

Open Learning Fire Service
Program
Federal Emergency Management
Agency (FEMA)
National Fire Academy
16825 South Seton Avenue
Emmitsburg, MD 21727

Oral Roberts University
External Degree Program
ORU Center for LifeLong
Education
7777 South Lewis
Tulsa, OK 74171

The Pennsylvania State
University
Department of Independent
Learning
128 Mitchell Building
University Park, PA 16802

Prescott College
Adult Degree Program
220 Grove Avenue
Prescott, AZ 86301

Regis University
University Without Walls
3333 Regis Boulevard
Denver, CO 80221

Roger Williams College
The Open Program
Bristol, RI 02809

Roosevelt University
External Degree Program
430 South Michigan Avenue
Chicago, IL 60605

Saint Joseph's College
External Degree Program
Windham, ME 04062

Saint Mary-of-the-Woods College
Women's External Degree (WED)
   Program
Saint Mary-of-the-Woods, IN 47876

Saint Mary's College of Minnesota
Minneapolis Graduate Center
2510 Park Avenue South
Minneapolis, MN 55404

Salve Regina University
Graduate Extension Study
100 Ochre Point Avenue
Newport, RI 02840

Saybrook Institute
Graduate School and Research
   Center
1550 Sutter Street
San Francisco, CA 94109

Skidmore College
University Without Walls
Saratoga Springs, NY 12866

Southeastern College of the
   Assemblies of God
Continuing Education Office
1000 Longfellow Boulevard
Lakeland, FL 33801

Southeastern University
Distance Learning Degree
   Program
501 Eye Street SW
Washington, DC 20024

Southwestern Adventist College
Adult Degree Program
Keene, TX 76059

Southwestern Assemblies of God
   College
1200 Sycamore
Waxahachie, TX 75165

State University System of Florida
   External Degree Program
Bachelor of Independent Studies
   (BIS)
University of South Florida
Tampa, FL 33620

Stephens College Without Walls
Campus Box 2083
Columbia, MO 65215

Syracuse University
Independent Study Degree
   Programs
University College
610 East Fayette Street
Syracuse, NY 13244

Teachers College/Columbia
   University
525 West 120th Street
Box 50
New York, NY 10027

Thomas Edison State College
101 West State Street
Trenton, NJ 08608

Trinity College
The Individualized Degree
   Program (IDP)
Hartford, CT 06106

Troy State University in
   Montgomery
External Degree Program
P.O. Drawer 4419
Montgomery, AL 36103

The Union Institute
440 East McMillan Street
Cincinnati, OH 45206

University of Alabama
New College External Degree
   Program
P.O Box 870182
University, AL 35487

University of Idaho
Engineering Outreach
Moscow, ID 83843

University of Iowa
Center for Credit Programs
116 International Center
Iowa City, IA 52242

University of Maryland
   University College
Open Learning Program
University Blvd. at Adelphi Road
College Park, MD 20742

University of Minnesota
Division of Health Services
   Administration
C-309, Box 97 Mayo Building
420 Delaware Street SE
Minneapolis, MN 55455

University of Missouri-Columbia
College of Agriculture
Nontraditional Study Program
126 Gentry Hall
Columbia, MO 65211

University of Nevada, Reno
Division of Continuing Education
206 Midby Byron Building
Reno, NV 89557

University of North Carolina at
   Chapel Hill
School of Public Health
Department of Health Policy &
   Administration
CB #7400, McGavran-Greenberg
   Hall
Chapel Hill, NC 27599

University of Oklahoma
College of Liberal Studies
1700 Asp Avenue, Suite 226
Norman, OK 73037-0001

University of Phoenix
4615 East Elwood Street
P.O. Box 52069
Phoenix, AZ 85040

University of Phoenix
Online Program Administrative
   Offices
101 California Street, Suite 505
San Francisco, CA 94111

University of Pittsburgh
University External Studies
   Program (UESP)
3808 Forbes Avenue
Pittsburgh, PA 15260

University of the State of
  New York
Regents College
1450 Western Avenue
Albany, NY 12203

University of Wisconsin-Madison
Department of Engineering
  Progessional Development
432 North Lake Street
Room 725
Madison, WI 53706

University of Wisconsin-
  Platteville
Extended Degree Program
  in Business Administration
506 Pioneer Tower
1 University Plaza
Platteville, WI 53818

University of Wisconsin-
  River Falls
Extended Degree Program
College of Agriculture
River Falls, WI 54022

University of Wisconsin-Superior
Extended Degree Program
1800 Grand Avenue
Superior, WI 54880

Upper Iowa University
Continuing Studies
P.O. Box 1861
Fayette, IA 52142

Vermont College of Norwich
  University
Montpelier, VT 05602

Walden University
801 Anchor Rode Drive
Naples, FL 33940

Weber State University
Outreach Education Program
School of Allied Health Sciences
Ogden, UT 84408

West Virginia University Regents
B.A. Degree Program
The Office of the Coordinator
206 Student Services Center
Morgantown, WV 26506

Organizations

Most of these organizations, businesses, or institutions can provide you with printed information about educational choices.

National Association of College
  Admission Counselors
1800 Diagonal Road, Suite 430
Alexandria, VA 22313
703-836-2222

Supplies information, much of it free, about the college admissions process.

National Institute of Independent
  Colleges and Universities
122 C Street, NW, Suite 750
Washington, DC 20001
202-347-7520

Mainly a professional association; they can refer you to other agencies.

Higher Education Information
Center
Boston Public Library
666 Boylston Street
Boston, MA 02116
617-536-0200

Arranges information on higher education the way a library does: topic by topic. The collection is comprehensive.

American Association for Higher
Education
One Dupont Circle, NW, Suite 600
Washington, DC 20036
202-293-6440

Serves as a resource for colleges and universities themselves.

American College Testing Program
P.O. Box 168
Iowa City, IA 52243
319-337-1000

Disseminators of the ACT test and other exams.

American Legion
700 North Pennsylvania Street
Indianapolis, IN 46206
317-635-8411

Veterans should write or call for free information.

American Association of Bible
Colleges
Box 1523
Fayetteville, AR 72702
501-521-8164

Bible colleges are a distinct category: They mainly grant divinity degrees.

American Association of
Community and Junior Colleges
One Dupont Circle, NW, Suite 410
Washington, DC 20036
202-293-7050

If you're wondering which community college offers baseball scholarships, or has technical programs, this association can help.

American Association of State
Colleges and Universities
One Dupont Circle, NY, Suite 700
Washington, DC 20036
202-939-9300

This is a resource if you're targeting mainly state institutions.

Junior Engineering Technical
Society (JETS)
345 East 47th Street
New York, NY 10017
212-705-7690

Administers an exam to high school students, the results of which are shared with engineering programs across the country.

National Association of Independent
Colleges and Universities
122 C Street, NW
Washington, DC 20001
202-347-7512

Women's College Coalition
1101 17th Street, NW
Washington, DC 20036
202-466-5430

There is a small but assertive number of colleges that admit only women.

American Association for Adult
and Continuing Education
1112 16th Street, NW, Suite 420
Washington, DC 20036
202-463-6333

*This is one of your best re-
sources for information about
post-secondary opportunities.*

American Council on Education
One Dupont Circle, NW
Washington, DC 20036
202-939-9300

*If you have questions about edu-
cational policy, contact the ACE.*

National Commission for
Cooperative Education
360 Huntington Avenue
Boston, MA 02115
617-437-3778

*"Earn as you learn" is offered
at the college as well as high
school level. You hold a job in your
field for academic credit.*

American Association for Retired
Persons
1090 K Street NW
Washington, DC 20049

*AARP is very active in promot-
ing educational opportunities for
members.*

National Council on Aging
600 Maryland Avenue, SW
Washington, DC 20024

*This organization and the one
following can help you with finding
day-care for elderly family members,
if your schedule requires you to be in
class.*

National Association for Family
Dare Care Providers
725 15th Street NW, Suite 505
Washington, DC 20005

National Association of Child Care
Resource and Referral Agencies
2116 Campus Drive SE
Rochester, MN 55904

Aspira of America, Inc. (Young
Puerto Ricans)
114 East 28th Street
New York, NY 10016

*Puerto Ricans receive benefits
of advice and financial assistance.*

National Society for Internships
and Experiential Education
3509 Haworth Drive, Suite 207
Raleigh, NC 27609

*If you have, or want, on-the-job
experience, find out ways it can be
incorporated into your education.*

National Action Council for
Minorities in Engineering
(NACME)
3 West 35th Street
New York, NY 10001
212-279-2626

*Minorities are underrepresent-
ed in engineering: NACME re-
cruits potential candidates.*

National Hispanic Scholarship
Fund
P.O. Box 748
San Francisco, CA 94101

*Financial assistance for Lati-
nos going to school.*

National Puerto Rican Forum
159 Washington Street
Hartford, CT 06106

An issues-oriented agency that focuses on Puerto Rican Americans.

National Scholarship Service and
Fund for Negro Students
(NSSFNS)
965 Martin Luther King Jr. Drive
Atlanta, GA 30314
404-577-3990

Financial assistance offered to African-Americans.

National Urban League
500 East 62nd Street
New York, NY 10021
212-326-1118

The National Urban League maintains a special office to deal with educational problems and opportunities.

Association for Children and
Adults with Learning
Disabilities (ACLD)
4156 Library Road
Pittsburgh, PA 15234
412-341-1515

Association for the Advancement
of Rehabilitation Technology
1101 Connecticut Ave. NW, Ste. 700
Washington, DC 20036
202-857-1199

This association, and the two following, provide information and referrals for Americans with disabilities.

Association on Handicapped
Student Service Programs in
Postsecondary Education
(AHSSPPE)
P. O. Box 21192
Columbus, OH 43221
614-488-4972

The College Board ATP Services
for Handicapped Students
Institutional Services
P.O. Box 592
Princeton, NJ 08541
609-771-7137

Division of Student Services
Programs
Special Services Branch
P.O. Box 23772
L'Enfant Plaza Station
Washington, DC 20026
202-732-4804

If you have questions about services you believe you should receive, this federal agency can help answer your questions.

Helen Keller National Center for
Deaf/Blind Youths and Adults
111 Middle Neck Road
Sands Point, NY 11050
516-844-8900

Higher Education and Adult
Training for People with Handicaps (HEATH) Resource Center
1 Dupont Circle, NW
Washington, DC 20036
202-939-9320
800-544-3284

National Information Center for
   Children and Youth with
   Handicaps (NICCYH)
P.O. Box 1492
Washington, DC 20013
703-893-6061

National Institute on Disability
   and Rehabilitation Research
Department of Educaiton
400 Maryland Avenue, SW
Washington, DC 20202
202-651-5000

National Library Service for the
   Blind and Physically
   Handicapped
Library of Congress
1291 Taylor Street, NW
Washington, DC 20542
202-707-5100

National Rehabilitation
   Information Center
8455 Colesville Road
Suite 935
Silver Spring, MD 20910
301-588-9284

National Technical Institute for
   the Deaf (NTID)
Rochester Institute of Technology
1 Lomb Memorial Drive
Rochester, NY 14623
716-475-6219

Recording for the Blind, Inc.
20 Roszel Road
Princeton, NJ 08542
609-452-0606

American Association of College
   Registrars and Admission
   Officers
1 Dupont Circle
Washington, DC 20036
202-293-9161

This association disseminates information about admissions and records policies and procedures.

Council on International
   Educational Exchange (CIEE)
205 East 42nd Street
New York, NY 10017
212-695-0291

This organization, and the four following, can provide you with information about living and studying abroad.

Experiment in International
   Living
P.O. Box 676
Brattleboro, VT 05302
802-257-7751

Institute of International
   Education (IEE)
809 United Nations Plaza
New York, NY 10017
212-883-8200

National Association for Foreign
   Student Affairs (NAFSA)
1860 19th Street NW
Washington, DC 20009
202-462-4811

Office of International Education
1717 Massachusetts Avenue NW
Washington, DC 20036
202-332-7134

U.S. Immigration and
   Naturalization Service
4420 North Fairfax Drive
Arlington, VA 22203
202-514-2000

Financial aid forms require that you supply information about your status as a resident in the United States. If you have questions or difficulties, contact the INS.

The College Board (and The Office of Adult Learning Services)
45 Columbus Avenue
New York, NY 10023
212-713-8000

The College Board is the organization that administers the SAT and can also send you free information about post-high school education from the office below.

Regional Information Office of Federal Student Aid

The following federal offices make available free publications to residents in the region about post-high school opportunities.

U.S. Department of Education
John W. McCormack Post Office
   and Courthouse
Room 536, Post Office Square
Boston, MA 02109
617-223-9317

U.S. Department of Education
26 Federal Plaza, Room 36-120
New York, NY 10278
212-264-7005

U.S. Department of Education
3535 Market Street
Room 16350
Philadelphia, PA 19104
215-596-1001

U.S. Department of Education
101 Marietta Tower Building
P.O. Box 1777
Atlanta, GA 30301
404-331-2502

U.S. Department of Education
401 South State St., Suite 700A
Chicago, IL 60605
312-353-5215

U.S. Department of Education
1200 Main Tower Bldg., Rm. 2125
Dallas, TX 75202
214-767-3626

U.S. Department of Education
10220 North Executive Hills Blvd.
9th Floor
P.O. Box 901381
Kansas City, MO 64190-1381
816-891-7972

U.S. Department of Education
Federal Office Building
1961 Stout Street
Room 380
Denver, CO 80294
303-844-3544

U.S. Department of Education
50 United Nations Plaza
Room 205
San Francisco, CA 94102
415-556-4920

U.S. Department of Education
Office of the Secretary of Regional
  Representatives
Jackson Federal Building
915 2nd Avenue, Room 3362
Seattle, WA 98174-1099
206-442-0460

Glossary

Academic year

The aggregate of annual study terms of a college or university, usually extending from the opening of classes each August or September through final examinations and graduation in the spring. Commonly, the academic year of an American college consists of two semesters or three quarters, followed by an additional summer session (with possible short intersessions) of course offerings.

Accreditation

Approval by a recognized accrediting organization of a college or university, or a study program, for meeting specified minimum standards of quality in its instruction, staffing, facilities, financial stability and policies. Professional accreditation applies to the study program or programs in a specific career field or academic subject and is typically granted by a major national professional or academic society in that field or discipline. State accreditation or approval of a college usually represents a minimum level of quality assurance and is required for a college or university to offer instruction to the public.

Achievement tests

College Board tests in specific college preparatory subjects. Required by some colleges for admission and used also in course placement.

American College Testing Program Assessment (ACT)

The test battery of the American College Testing Program. Required for admission by many colleges and universities.

Application for Federal Student Aid

A form that may be used by students applying for federally sponsored financial aid, chiefly Pell Grants and Guaranteed Student Loans.

Associate degree

The degree granted by a college or university for completion of a study program normally taking two years of full-time study (or longer, if part-time study.)

Career services office or center

A college office or department providing services to assist students in choosing careers, in developing skills in searching and qualifying for jobs—and in actually finding and obtaining jobs. The office provides listings of job openings and interviews with corporate and government recruiters visiting the campus. Such an office might also be identified as a placement bureau, student placement office or career resources center.

Challenge examinations

Examinations offered by a college that are prepared in specific subjects by its own faculty members and that enable students to earn credits by passing the examinations instead of attending class sessions.

College Board

An education association whose members include colleges and secondary schools. It provides college entrance examinations (including the Scholastic Aptitude Test and Achievement Tests) and has a constituent association, the College Scholarship Service. Many testing and scholarship services of the Board are administered by Educational Testing Service (ETS), a nonprofit education organization.

College-Level Examination Program (CLEP)

A College Board program of examinations in undergraduate college subjects. Widely used by colleges to award degree credit to students for nontraditional college-level learning. See credit by examination.

College Scholarship Service (CSS)

An association of the College Board offering services designed to provide for the distribution of financial aid funds to college students by determining each student's financial need.

College Work-Study Program (CWSP)

A federally sponsored financial aid program that provides jobs for students with demonstrated financial need.

Contract learning program

A college study program in which the student studies independently and at periodic intervals (such as every few months) makes a learning agreement or contract with a faculty adviser, which defines the learning to be carried out during the term of that agreement or contract.

Cooperative work-study program

A study program offered by more than 900 colleges in which the student alternates between periods of full-time study and full-time employment in a field related to the study area, such as engineering or business administration.

Correspondence study course

A course (which can be one recognized for degree credit and conducted by a regionally accredited college) for which the student registers and receives and sends course materials by mail, and in which the student learns independently without class attendance (usually proceeding on a lesson-by-lesson basis with lesson assignments guided, graded and returned by a teacher assigned to the student for the course).

Credit

Unit widely used by colleges to specify amounts of study that a student must complete with satisfactory performance in order to qualify for an academic degree. Generally, a course meeting one hour a week through a semester carries one semester-hour credit, a course meeting two hours a week carries two semester-hour credits, and so on. A total of at least 120 credits is required for a bachelor's degree, and at least 60 credits are required for an associate degree. Colleges operating on a quarter calendar use a similar system based on quarter-hour credits, with three quarter-hour credits usually equivalent to two semester-hour credits.

Credit by examination

Credit toward a degree awarded by a college on the basis of a student's performance on specified examinations (such as a college's own challenge examinations or those of the College-Level Examination Program).

Educational Testing Service (ETS)

See College Board.

Elective course

A course that a student takes by choice as distinguished from a course specifically required for a degree.

Equivalency diploma

A diploma officially recognized as a certificate of high school graduation. Earned by passing specified examinations, usually the General Educational Development (GED) tests, rather than through customary high school attendance.

Experiential learning credit

(also called life experience credit). Credit awarded by a college for college-level learning acquired by a student in previous experience at work or in other activities.

External degree program

A study program or set of study programs offered by a college in which a student can earn a degree with little or no attendance at the college (often, through some combination of credit by examination, transfer credit, experiential learning credit, independent study and credit for prior coursework outside colleges).

Financial Aid Form (FAF)

The financial information collection form used by the College Scholarship Service in determining a student's financial need. The Free Application for Federal Student Aid (FAFSA) has replaced the FAF. However, some colleges still require it. Check with the admissions office.

Financial need

The difference between what the student and her/his spouse (or parents) can afford to spend toward that student's college costs and the total of those costs, as computed in the need analysis systems used by colleges and other aid sponsors. In those systems, colleges and other sponsors require aid applicants to complete family financial information collection forms to provide basic data for computations.

Free Application for Federal Student Aid

(FAFSA). See Financial Aid Form. The FAFSA is available each year in November in high school guidance offices and college financial aid offices.

4-1-4 academic year calendar

A variant of the two-semester academic year calendar in which the academic year consists of a four-month fall semester, a one-month winter intersession, and a four-month spring semester.

Full-time study

The enrollment status of a student who is registered for at least 12 semester-hour credits (or at least 18 quarter-hour credits) per term of the regular academic year, as usually defined by colleges. Part-time student is the enrollment status of students registered for fewer credits per term than the minimum set by the college for full-time study.

General Educational Development (GED) tests

A series of five tests that adults who did not complete high school may take to qualify for an equivalency diploma.

Grade point average (GPA)

A numerical index of overall student academic performance. It is calculated by first multiplying the number of credits earned in each completed course by the numerical value of the student's grade in that course (generally A=4, B=3, C=2, D=1, and E or F = 0). All the resulting grade points for each course are then added, and their sum is divided by the total number of credits taken. (A student who has earned A grades in all courses will have a GPA of 4.0, for example.) For high school GPAs, the number of class hours or periods per week for each course is used instead of the number of credits earned for the course.

Graduate study program, graduate degree

A study program for which a bachelor's degree or the equivalent is usually required for admission; a degree earned through a graduate study program.

Guaranteed student loan (GSL) Program

A federally sponsored program of financial aid in which students may take out loans for college costs at subsidized interest rates.

Independent study

A program that does not require class attendance for degree credit. The student learns independently under the supervision of a faculty member.

Life experience credit

See Experiential learning credit.

Major

The subject or career field that serves as the area concentration in the student's study program for a degree. For a bachelor's degree, students must commonly earn about one-fourth of their credits in the major.

Ombudsperson

The administrative officer at some colleges whose major duties are to receive and rectify grievances reported by students.

Part-time study

See Full-time study.

Pell Grant Program

A federally sponsored program of financial aid in which college students may qualify for grants adjusted in amount according to financial need.

Placement office

See Career services office.

Proficiency Examination Program (PEP)

A program of examinations in undergraduate college subjects widely used by colleges to award degree credit to students by examination, and offered by the American College Testing Program. See Credit by examination.

Quarter

See Academic year.

Registration

For a college academic term, the process by which the student chooses, enrolls in and pays for course sessions for the term; also, the period of several days before the term opening designated by the college for carrying out that process. For entrance tests required by a college for admission, the process by which the student chooses and enrolls for (and pays for) the test date and test center location at which to take the test or tests.

Requirements

For a college degree, the amounts and kinds of study stipulated by the college as necessary in order to qualify for that degree. For college admission, the documents, test results, and possibly minimum qualifications and interview, stipulated by the college as necessary in order to qualify for admission.

Scholastic Aptitude Test (SAT)

A test of verbal and mathematical reasoning abilities that is required for admission by many colleges and universities and is offered by the College Board.

Supplemental Educational Opportunity Grant (SEOG) program

A federally sponsored program of financial aid providing grant assistance and administered by colleges, and for which high-need students may qualify automatically if they have applied for both federal and college aid.

Terminal study program

A study program usually offered by a two-year community college that is designed to qualify students for immediate employment upon completing the program rather than for transfer to a bachelor's degree program. Many terminal programs lead to an associate degree.

Transcript

An official record of the courses taken and grades earned by a student throughout high school or in college.

Transfer credit

Credit accepted by a college toward a degree on the basis of prior study by the student at another college.

Transfer program

A study program usually offered by a two-year community college that is designed to qualify students completing the program for transfer to a bachelor's degree program with little or no loss of credit. Most transfer programs lead to an associate degree.

Trimester

An alternate name for semester employed by colleges that offer year-round study. Three trimesters make up one year (with the third trimester representing the summer sessions).

Undergraduate

Pertaining to studies for associate or bachelor's degrees.

Upper-division

Pertaining to studies on the level of the junior and senior years of study for a bachelor's degree (the last two years of study for a bachelor's, in conventional full-time study programs).

Weekend college study program

A study program designed especially for working adults in which students attend course sessions primarily or entirely during weekends. In many such programs, the student may be able to earn a degree in as few years as students in conventional full-time programs leading to that degree.

Work-study

See Cooperative work-study program and College Work-Study Program.

Conclusion

When I started writing this book, I was enrolling in my first class since 1979 (my experiences going back to school gave me the idea for the book: I figured I must be pretty typical). As I wrote the chapters, one at at time, I was moving through a series of eight courses having to do with school administration. So rest assured—the tips I've given here are ones I've "road-tested" on my own!

Now, the big question: Has it paid off? Let me give you the pros and cons:

It's been tough commuting back and forth. There were many nights driving home at 9:30 p.m. when I realized I still had some chores waiting for me, and all I really wanted to do was go to bed. Likewise, my two kids got a little tired of hearing how I had to study, or I had a test coming up and I had to prepare for it. My son began prefacing his conversations to me with, "What's the schedule for today?" Or, "Do you have to work at the computer?" He decided to save his breath if a request was going to be met with, "I'd like to, Andrew, but I've got work to do."

Finally, I felt the physical strain, too. I remember one afternoon about 5:30 p.m., sitting at a desk listening to a lecture. I kept scribbling out words I'd misspelled as I tried to listen and take notes. At 5:45, I wrote in the margin: "Too tired to write anymore."

Now the upside...

I went back to school because I was promoted to the head of my department. It was an unusual situation. The job description was rewritten so that the position didn't require a background in supervision—just experience and ideas.

Within the first two weeks, however, I realized that no amount of "good ideas" and pleasantry was going to solve some of the managerial problems that kept cropping up. So I enrolled in school again.

There were two immediate benefits. First, I was in classes with people in exactly the same situation as I was. Nearly everyone was making a career move and needed more education. Most of our questions in class had to do with specific problems: "I had to make a decision yesterday whether to buy a new piece of equipment and..." It was reassuring and helpful to hear so many other adults finding their way.

Second, I realized that many of the situations I was encountering at work were not unusual. In other words, the disagreements, policy changes, procedural questions, personal conflicts, communication breakdowns—practically all of it—were to be expected. It was not of my doing (well, okay—sometimes it was). But with the skills I was learning, I found that I became more comfortable and better at my work.

I guess it's not bragging to say I became more successful.

And that's the point of going back to school. It's not just to fill your head with more information. You could read a stack of books instead, if that were the purpose. The goal is to become more effective. The case studies instructors give you, the small group discussions, the panel presentations by class members really show you the shortcuts to success.

Now the rest of it is up to you. No certificate, no diploma will automatically make a positive difference in your life.

But you can bet on this: The more education you have, the farther you'll go.

Keep that in mind—because who knows? You might find you need to go back to school *again* so you can go even farther.

Index